HOW TO "READ" MANGA

GLOOM
グルームパーティー
PARTY

川島よしお
YOSHIO KAWASHIMA

1

Translation & Adaptation . . . . .G Genki
Layout . . . . .John Ott
Print Production . . . . .Mr. Fred
Publisher . . . . .Hikaru Sasahara

Gloom Party 1 © Yoshio Kawashima 1996. Originally published in Japan in 1996 by Akita Publishing Co., Ltd. English translation rights arranged with Akita Publishing Co., Ltd. through TOHAN CORPORATION, TOKYO. All rights reserved. English translation copyright © 2006 by DIGITAL MANGA, Inc. All other material © 2006 by DIGITAL MANGA, Inc. All rights reserved. No portion of this publication may be reproduced or transmitted in any form or by any means without written permission from the copyright holders. Any likeness of characters, places, and situations featured in this publication to actual persons (living or deceased), events, places, and situations is purely coincidental. All characters depicted in sexually explicit scenes in this publication are at least the age of consent or older. The DMP logo is ™ of DIGITAL MANGA, Inc.

English Edition Published by
DIGITAL MANGA PUBLISHING
A division of **DIGITAL MANGA, Inc.**
1487 W. 178th Street, Suite 300
Gardena, CA 90248

www.dmpbooks.com

First Edition: January 2006
ISBN: 1-56970-956-4

10 9 8 7 6 5 4 3 2 1

Printed in China

GLOOM PARTY

1

YOSHIO KAWASHIMA

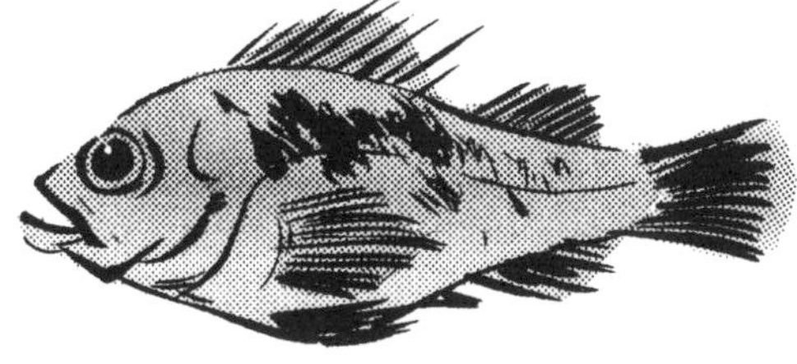

Translation and commentary by:

G. Genki

Los Angeles

ALWAYS BUSY WITH ZUWAI CRABS.

● This is dedicated to Y Marine Products, Tama Branch.

シリーズ

ひとコマ番外地(ばんがいち)

Series

Irregular One Panel Page

① *Blurb:* Cheap!! Delicious!!

② (Kounago)

③ A little princess who sells Kounago.

④ *Girl:* Yummy

Commentary:

• Because this book consists of four panel comic strips, this page, which has only one panel, is an irregularity. The author named this page "One Panel 番外地 (Bangaichi)." 番外地 (Bangaichi) represents "Number Outside Location" (i.e. the address is irregular).

• こうなご (kounago) is a type of small fish perfect for a tempura dish. こうなご (kounago) in Kanji is 小女子 (kounago). Kanji characters 小女子 (kounago) represent "small girl child." Meanwhile, 小公女 (shôkôjo) is written in Kanji that represent "small public girl" which translate to "little princess." It's obvious the author played with the words here because there's a strong similarity between 小女子 (kounago) and 小公女 (shôkôjo). The joke lies in the contrasting meanings of the similar Kanji.

こしぼね 腰骨グリグリ

HIP BONE GURI GURI

Ms. Itoh: This is punishment for being naughty!!!
Student: No! Not the Guri Guri—please!

Principal: What are you doing, Ms. Itoh?
Ms. Itoh: It's Hip Bone Guri Guri, Principal...

Principal: I've never heard of that before ...
FX: Guri guri
Ms. Itoh: Would you like to try some, Principal?
FX: (kya ha ha, hee hee hee hee, ha ha ha) *Laughing uncontrollably.*

Ms. Itoh: How is it?
FX: Guri guri
Principal: Oh, it's good. It's unbelievably good. Uh, ha ha ha

せんせい モーレツ先生

MOHRETSU SENSEI

Student: Good morning, Sensei! Kya!
FX: (do do do do do) *A loud sound reminiscent of a stampede.*

FX: (do do do do do do do do) *A loud sound reminiscent of a stampede.*
Student: No! It's so Mohretsu.

FX: (ta ta ta ta) *A light sound of someone running.*

Sensei: When you're wearing a skirt, don't wear shorts!!!
FX: (pan) *Slap*

Commentary:

• グリグリ(guri guri) is the sensation of something hard moving smoothly inside.

• Here, Ms. Itoh's hip bones are moving smoothly inside her buns, making them a perfect massaging tool.

• おしおき (oshioki) literally means "punishment." It is sometimes used to mean "giving sexual stimulation."

• Although Ms. Itoh says it's おしおき (i.e., non-sexual punishment), it obviously has a double meaning and that's where the humor lies.

Commentary:

• モーレツ (mohretsu) can be written in Kanji as 猛烈. It is a word that means aggressive and wildly violent.

• 先生 (sensei) is a commonly used term for addressing someone with respect. Usually, it's used to address people like teachers, professors, lawyers, doctors and politicians.

• 先生 (sensei) is running past the female students in a モーレツ (mohretsu) fashion, creating a whirlwind as he tries to catch a glimpse of their panties. You may see a parallel between the imagery used here and the famous picture of Marilyn Monroe with her skirt flying up. Also please note that there was a popular TV commercial in Japan that used similar imagery. This ad featured Rosa Ogawa with her skirt flying up.

• Sensei is angry when one of the students turns out to be wearing shorts, which prevents him from seeing her underwear. His anger is what makes this so funny.

よっ!! エッチだね!!

YOH, IT'S ECCHI!

Man: Yoh! Ecchi! Ecchi!
Man: It's ecchi!
FX: (pii pii pii) *Whistling hard.*

Girl: No!!
FX: (pakkon pakkon) *Up and down. Up and down.*

FX: (pako pako) *Up and down. Up and down.*
FX: (pita) *Suddenly silent.*

Man: Yoh! Ecchi!
Man: Ecchi!
Man: It's ecchi!
Girl: No!
FX: (pako pako pako) *Up and down. Up and down.*

Commentary:

• エッチ(ecchi) is the Japanese pronunciation for the letter "H." This エッチ(ecchi) is derived from a Japanese word 破廉恥 (harenchi), which means infamy, shamelessness, ignominy or effrontery. When people say エッチ(ecchi), it usually has something to do with sex or lust.

• The men are teasing the girl because it looks as if she's having sex when she moves up and down on the horse.

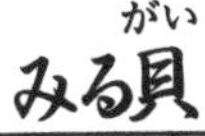

GIANT CLAM

Customer: Giant clam please.
Sushi Chef: Er— Yes...

FX: (doki doki doki doki) *Throbbing of her heart—frightened or feeling tense from the suspense.*

Sushi Chef: Kya!!
FX: (pyuu) *A sound of something spurting out.*
FX: (jiiin) *Impressed.*

Sushi Chef: What would you like next...?
Customer: Giant clam please.

Commentary:

• みる貝 (miru-gai) is the Japanese word for a type of clam (a giant clam) often used for sushi. みる (miru), however, sounds the same as the word 見る(miru) which means look or watch. 貝 (kai or gai) is the word that means clam, but it also sounds the same as 甲斐 (kai) that means "worth" something.

• The customer finds it worthwhile to watch the female sushi chef handle the giant clam. The way she approaches the clam is timid and nervous. She's blushing too—just like a virgin. This is what makes it funny. When she picks up the みる貝 (miru-gai) and it spurts, we know exactly what the man is thinking.

• Also, take note that きゃっ (kya) is a short scream, showing the girl's surprise and naiveté.

せんせい 先生!!! — SENSEI!!!

先生は悲しいぞ!! カツアゲなんて!!

でもよう先生… たったの500円だぜ

Sensei: I'm very disappointed. How come it's just a deep-fried cutlet?
Student: But, Sensei... Only 500 yen, you know.

Sensei: It's got nothing to do with money..
Student: Wow, she's a beauty!

Sensei: Ge he he, Neh-chan.
Sensei: Ge he he, Neh-chan. Ge he he.

Sensei: It's got nothing to do with money!!!
FX: (baki) Thud *(a heavy blow).*

Commentary:

• 先生 (sensei) apparently asked the student to go buy him some lunch. He's disappointed that the student bought a deep-fried cutlet. When a good looking woman walks by, 先生 (sensei) tries to make a pass at her.

• げっへっへ (ge he he) is the sound of a sleazy laugh. ねえちゃん (neh-chan) is a term used for addressing an older sister, but it can also be used to address a female stranger in a (sometimes overly) friendly way.

• After 先生 (sensei) winds up with lumps on his head, he repeats the same line as before: "It's got nothing to do with money!!" Only this time it has a double meaning. It's not just him resuming his conversation with the student. Instead, it's him insisting that a woman should not reject a man just because he's poor.

コーチ!!! — COACH!!!

FX: (kuru kuru kuru kuru) *Spin*

FX: (za) *Sudden stop*

Girl: I did it, coach! I did three and a half spins successfully!
FX: (ba) Dramatically.

Coach: How many times do I have to tell you not to wear shorts underneath!
FX: (pan pan) *Slap, slap*

Commentary:

• コーチ(kôchi) is "coach." コーチ(kôchi) is very disappointed that he didn't get to see her panties.

• This comic strip is all about how Japanese girls wear shorts called ブルマ (buruma) to hide their panties from boys. ブルマ (buruma) are commonly used girls' shorts for gym classes. The comic implies that by wearing them outside the gym classes, girls take the fun out by preventing the boys from catching a glimpse of their panties.

• The one entitled MOHRETSU SENSEI also uses the Japanese cultural reference to ブルマ (buruma) .

プレリュード

PRELUDE

Yuka: I'm Yuka. Fifteen years old.

Yuka: Let me show you my secret.

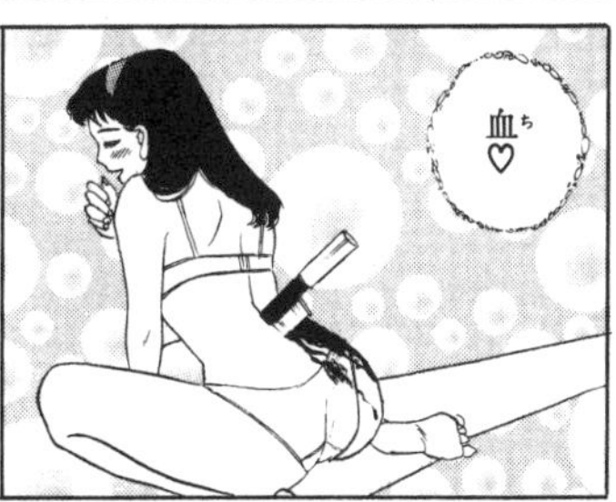

Yuka: Blood.

Yuka: I'm embarrassed.

Commentary:

• What's so odd and funny about this comic strip is the way in which her secret is revealed. She talks in a shy, naïve and light manner. Once her secret is revealed, she becomes embarrassed. It's as if her secret is her period—not the knife in her back that's making her bleed.

兄貴!!

BIG BRO!

Man: What a tight-lipped woman you are. This'll be your last chance!!
Woman: What do you mean?

Man: Big Bro!! It's your turn!
FX: (doohn) *Tah-dah*

Woman: Oh no. Not this sticky, wet stuff!
FX: (nuru nuru) *Slippery*
FX: (nuto nuto) *Sticky*
Woman: Let me go!

Man: It's interesting in its own way...!
Woman: Let me go!
Woman: Haan.
Woman: No, don't.

Commentary:

• The Japanese word used for "let me go" is ゆるして (yurushite). It means "pardon me" or "forgive me." Please look at the comic strip HIP BONE GURI GURI, where it describes the use of the word おしおき (oshioki). The word ゆるして (yurushite) is often used by a person begging "to be pardoned or forgiven" by someone who is inflicting some sort of おしおき (oshioki). The humor lies in the fact that when a person is sexually stimulated by おしおき (oshioki), its common to cry out ゆるして (yurushite) and beg for an end to the おしおき (oshioki). Usually this takes place in a sadomasochistic context, where a sadistic man is punishing a woman during sex.

• はあああん (haan) is a type of groan a sexually stimulated woman might make. You get the idea.

生鮮売場のひとコマ

A STORY AT THE FRESH PRODUCE MARKET

Customer: Will you cut up that live sea bream for me?
FX: (bichi bichi bichi) *Flopping fish*
Man: Alright.

Customer: I'd like some cow liver that can be prepared as sashimi.
Man: What?

Man: C'mon... Let's go...
Customer: W—Wait a second... You don't mean...

Cow: ...
FX: (jiii) *Staring hard*
FX: (poro poro) *Tears dripping*
Customer: Urrgh

Commentary:

• The ironic part of this comic strip is that the customer has no problem with the fish being killed right in front of her, but she finds it extremely disturbing to have the cow slaughtered in the same way.

有森・・・

ARIMORI

Girl: Kyaah. Look! Look!! There goes Arimori-san, the top student at school!
Boy: Arimori...?
FX: (da) *Dash*

Arimori: Sensei!!
Sensei: Oh, what's the matter, Arimori...?

Arimori: I answered almost everything wrong on this test. Why'd I get such a good score...?

Sensei: I wonder why. Ha ha ha ha ha.
Arimori: It's terrible. What've I done to you?

Sensei: You know... I like you best when you're on top, running wholeheartedly, without any hesitation...
Arimori: A u u u u

Girl: Kyaah. Look! Look!! There goes Arimori-san, the top student at school!
Boy: Arimori...?
FX: (da) *Dash*

Commentary:

- キャーッ (kyaah) is a female scream of delight.
- あううううう (auuuu) is a sobbing sound.
- The sadistic 先生 (sensei) enjoys giving Arimori-san good grades, especially when she doesn't deserve them, so that he can see her dash across school. Please note, there is an Olympic marathon runner representing Japan named Arimori. Marathons are popular nation-wide in Japan, and Arimori must carry the weight of the national expectation. With that knowledge, read between the lines and you'll understand the gag.

DAY TO BE MARRIED

Yoshiko: Even after I marry, I hope I can keep this teddy bear in my room.

Yoshiko: When I was a child, this teddy bear felt so big for me to hold onto, but...

Yoshiko: Now, it feels (so small)...

Yoshiko: I suppose I've grown up...

FX: (gyu) *Squeeze tightly*

Yoshiko: Oh no... I can't stop my tears...

Father: Yoshiko!! You've grown!! Yoshiko.

Commentary:

• 大きくなる (ookikunaru) means, when literally translated, "get bigger" or "gotten big." When the father used the term 大きくなる (ookikunaru), he meant that his daughter, Yoshiko, has grown up. The author played with the word to illustrate how, literally, Yoshiko has grown huge to match the literal meaning of the term 大きくなる (ookikunaru). The parents are drawn in an oddly small way to emphasize the point.

汗と涙

SWEAT AND TEARS

Sensei: Start!!

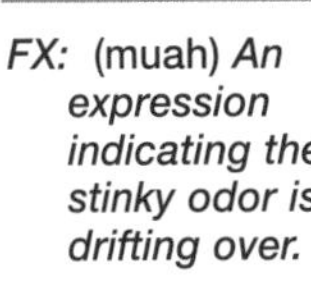

FX: (muah) *An expression indicating the stinky odor is drifting over.*

Girl: Gauntlet!!

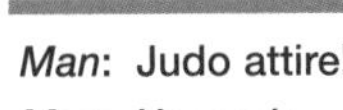

Man: Judo attire!

Man: Uryaaah

Girl: I can't take it anymore. I lose...

Man: What do you mean?

Sensei: What about your panties, the best weapon of all.

Girl: Why are you getting involved?

Sensei: Please reconsider!!

Sensei: Without the "panties soaked in sweat," there's no adolescence!!

Sensei: Uooooh

Girl: Kyaaah! Kyaaah!

Man: Waaaan

Commentary:

• 青春 (seishun) is a word used to describe the period of adolescence. The idea of 青春 (seishun) is often associated with sweat and tears in that, a person can't go through 青春 (seishun) without them. See how this comic strip is loaded with sweat and tears, making fun of the word 青春 (seishun)?

• うりゃああああ (uryaaah) is a Kiai-like yell of concentration, whileうおおおおお (uooooh) and わあああん (waaaan) are the sound of crying.

シリーズ
ひとコマ番外地（ばんがいち）

Series
Irregular One Panel Page

LAP PILLOW

Girl: It's kind'a indecent...

Commentary:

• ひざまくら (hizamakura) is a word meaning "the lap used as a pillow to rest one's head on." The idea of ひざまくら (hizamakura) usually conjures up a sense of comfort and warmth—like a mother letting her child rest or a wife letting her husband rest.

• やらしい (yarashii) comes from いやらしい (iyarashii) which means indecent.

• What's funny about this comic strip is that the idea of ひざまくら (hizamakura), which does not have any sexual nuances, is now placed in a sexual and sensual context.

春の陽だまりI

SUNNY SPRING DAY I

Boy: What a sunny, warm spring day...

FX: (poka poka poka poka poka) *Cozy, warm sunshine.*

Boy: I wonder why I'm getting an erection...

FX: (poka poka poka) *Cozy, warm sunshine.*

FX: (kin kin kin) *Hard-on.*

Boy: Just after lunch, we rise up, under the spring sunshine.

Boy: A bit too long.

Boy: What a sleepy day today...

FX: (poka poka poka poka poka) *Cozy, warm sunshine.*

春の陽だまりII

SUNNY SPRING DAY II

Boy: I've got to get my mind off that and make it stop...

FX: (poka poka) *Cozy, warm sunshine.*

FX: (doki doki) *Throbbing heart.*

FX: (moso moso) *Move about, trying to get comfortable.*

Boy: Let me think.

Boy: Let me see... in a situation like this...

Boy: if I was a girl, what would it be like...?

FX: (kin kin kin kin kin kin) *Hard-on.*

Boy: Urrgh

Commentary:

• In the panel #3, the boy is composing a traditional Japanese Haiku poem. The poem he composed doesn't fit within the 5-7-5 syllable rule, but instead, it comes out to 5-7-7, and that's why he says "(it's) a bit too long."

• ひま (hima) is the word the boy used to describe how he felt in panel #4. ひま (hima) means "no scheduled engagement (nothing to do)," "dull," or "free time." In this particular situation, however, he is at school, participating in class. He used the word ひま (hima) to express how bored he is—when he's not supposed to feel that way. I'm sure many readers can relate to how he feels.

Commentary:

• そうだ (souda) is a phrase used to express the point when one has come to a realization, remembered something, or come up with some new idea.

• The reason why we know that the boy is at school is because of the school uniform he's wearing, as well as the desks and chairs. They're all very typical of a classroom setup in Japan.

グルームパーティー
GLOOM PARTY

Father: He died in war.

Father: He was killed by the occupying army.

Father: He starved to death.

Mother: Stop it.

Son: He was killed riding his motorcycle.

Son: He also got killed in an accident.

Son: He died of AIDS.

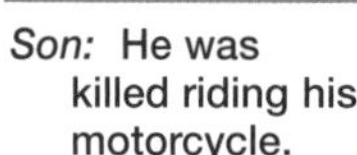

Mother: Like I said, stop it.

アルバムから
PHOTO ALBUM

Girl: Zipper's down.

Boy: Yup. That's my grandpa.

Girl: Zipper's down.

Boy: Yup. That's my dad.

Girl: Zipper's down.

Boy: Yup. Wanna go out to eat?

Sister: Hey, Onii-chan, I'm home.

Girl: ...

Boy: What do you wanna eat?

Commentary:

• Despite the change in social environment, Father and Son share a similar experience.

• From the panels #2 and #4, we can tell that the Father is apparently drinking 酒 (sake), Japanese rice wine, while the Mother and Son are drinking green tea. They are sitting around a typical こたつ (kotatsu). こたつ (kotatsu) is a type of table covered by a square futon comforter. A heating device is attached to the table, and it's used during the cold winter season as leg/body warmer.

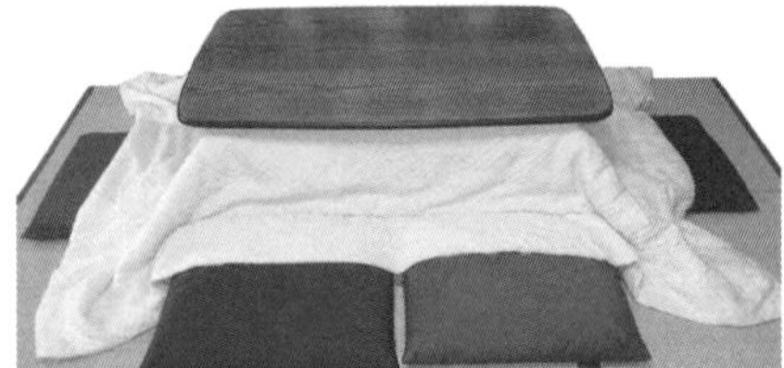

Kotatsu

Commentary:

• Obviously, for three generations, the males in the boy's family have not changed. They all have a problem keeping their front zipper up.

• The humor lies in the fact that the girl's attempt to communicate this has failed. This is because of the way the Japanese language allows for reading between lines to convey the true intent of the speaker. In addition, it's awkward to talk in specific and clear terms about something embarrassing like this, which only aggravates the miscommunication.

• This type of miscommunication would probably never occur in English—because, the non-Japanese girl would have said "your zipper is down," instead of simply saying "zipper's down."

転校生 (てんこうせい)

TRANSFER STUDENT

Teacher: Let me introduce the transfer student...

FX: (tsuka tsuka tsuka) *Brisk footsteps.*

Girl: How do you do, everyone.

よくわかんねえけどセクシーバディだっ!!!

Boy: Wakame-chan has come to our school.

Boy: I don't know what's going on, but she's got a sexy body!!!

Commentary:

• ワカメちゃん (Wakame-chan) is a well known anime character from the series called "サザエさん" (Sazae-san). The comic strip version ofサザエさん (Sazae-san) was started in 1949. The anime version of サザエさん (Sazae-san) began in 1969, and it's still on air. ワカメちゃん (Wakame-chan) is a perpetual nine-year-old, with her trademark haircut and mini-skirt with her panties showing.

• ワカメちゃん (Wakame-chan) appears in this comic strip as a teenager with her trademark haircut and mini-skirt with her panties showing. Many Japanese readers, who grew up with the series, will find it funny to visualize ワカメちゃん (Wakame-chan) as a grown up girl within this context.

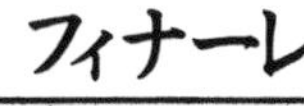

FINALE

Song: Chah, chalala, chararara, cha.

ババンバ バンバン バン♪

Girl: Lalan la lan lan lan.

Girl: Lalan la lan lan lan.

Girls: Lan lan!

Old man: Don't wear shorts.

FX: (tei) *Tut*

Commentary:

• ブルマ (buruma) are the shorts referred to in panel #4. The old man cannot stand seeing ブルマ (buruma) instead of the girl's panties.

• What's particularly funny about this comic strip is that the old man has an uncanny resemblance to a well-known Japanese star, いかりや長助 (Chousuke Ikariya). He recently passed away, but because of his long career with a show called "8 時だよ全員集合" (It's Eight O'clock! Let's get together, everyone!), most Japanese still remember him.

MARTINI

マティーニ♡

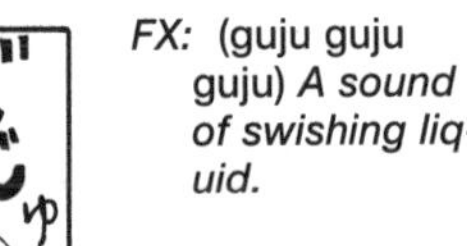

FX: (guju guju guju) *A sound of swishing liquid.*

Girl: Martini.

FX: (dori dori dori dori) *A sound of liquid dribbling down.*

FX: (gokyu gokyu gokyu) *A sound of downing the drink fast.*

Man: More please ♥

Commentary:

• おかわり (okawari) is a verb that means a person is asking for another serving of the same food/drink he/she has been previously served. おかわり (okawari) can also be used as a noun meaning that the item is being served again.

• If you can understand the middle-aged businessman's sentiments here, you'll get what the author is making fun of. If not, just say yuck and move on.

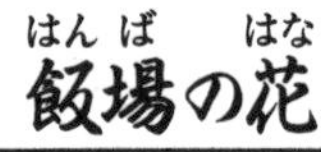

A FLOWER OF THE CONSTRUCTION CAMP

Worker: Boss!! She makes it difficult to work hard.

Boss: What? Even when she's a high school student and wearing a miniskirt?

Commentary:

• 花 (hana) means flower, but it can refer to a beautiful female that attracts attention. 飯場 (hanba) is a place where mine or construction workers temporarily live together on the site. Similar to the phrase 紅一点 (kouitten), 飯場の花 (hanbano hana) refers to a single woman among rough guys.

• 親方 (oyakata) means master, boss, chief or foreman. Although the word can be used in other situations, it's especially suited to the construction business.

• 親方 (oyakata) thought that having a sexy girl on the construction site might make the guys work harder, but instead, it backfires, distracting the workers from focusing on the work at hand. He should've known men's psychology better.

集中治療室

EMERGENCY ROOM

Kumiko: G-Grandpa!!

Mother: Grandpa, Kumiko just arrived.

Father: How dare you show up so late!

Mother: Please, not now...

Kumiko: Every-one's wearing the surgical gown backside front...

Doctor: He has just passed away...

Kumiko: Backside front...

Kumiko: Grandpa!!!

Kumiko: Backside front...

Commentary:

• Even at the most stressful time, when her grandfather has passes away, Kumiko can't help but think about the surgical gown being worn backside front.

• It's all about the dignity of life and death. What Kumiko felt is an innate human emotion, probably universal to any human being.

• As for what she sees when she lifts the blanket off of the deceased, I'll leave it up to your imagination.

バスの中 — ON THE BUS

Recording: The next stop is the XX Station, darling. ♥

Recording: Kids often spring out from that street corner.

Recording: The next stop is...

Driver: Thanks, Kah-chan!

Driver: Because of this tape, I haven't had an accident today.

Passenger: Don't play that weird tape!

FX: (poke) *A sound of the knock/punch.*

Commentary:

- When you ride a bus in Japan, you'll notice that a female recording is always played, letting the passengers know what the next station is. When a passenger's destination is announced, the passenger usually presses a nearby button to notify the driver so that the driver will stop the bus at the next bus stop.
- This comic strip twists this custom and creates a "what if" scenario.
- 母ちゃん (kah-chan) is usually used to address one's mother in an equivalent way to "Mom," but it can also be used by a husband to address his wife. In this situation, it's obvious that 母ちゃん (kah-chan) is the driver's wife—because otherwise, the recorded voice would not have used the word あなた (anata) in the panel #1. あなた (anata) literally means "you," but used within this context, it is meant as "darling."

のり子ッ!!! — NORIKO!!!

Someone: A hit and run!!

Father: N—Noriko!!

Father: What is it, Noriko?

Mother: Don't move, Noriko!!

Mother: "It hurts."

Father: "It hurts."

FX: (pyo-on pyo-on) *Hop up and down.*

Mother: You don't need to communicate using body language at a time like this!!

Father: What a wordless child you are, Noriko!

Commentary:

- のり子 (Noriko)'s parents are beside themselves after she was hit by a car. のり子 (Noriko) is apparently 無口 (mukuchi), and that means she is usually quiet and doesn't express her thoughts in words. 無口 (mukuchi) does not imply that she has a speech impediment, but rather that she prefers not to speak.
- What's funny about this comic strip is that even in an extreme situation, のり子 (Noriko)'s tendency to be 無口 (mukuchi) makes her unwilling to use words to communicate.
- The word 無口 (mukuchi) is made up of the Kanji characters that represents "non-existent mouth," thus, we can see that there is some underlying word play, showing what a child without a mouth would do to relate her feelings.

ALICE'S CHILD

FX: (ton ton ton ton ton) *The sound of chopping vegetables on a cutting board.*

FX: (koto koto koto) *The sound of boiling and cooking.*

Husband: Let me sneak up behind my bride, and...

FX: (ba) *The sound of sudden move.*

Wife: Kyaah, what're you doing?

Husband: It was my dream to try something like this. Wa ha ha ha ha.

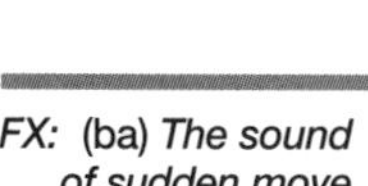

Husband: Don't you wear the shorts!

FX: (ban) *bang*

Wife: Kyaaah

先生の十八番 愛の鞭オシリペンペン

同窓会にて

Text: Sensei's Special Loving Whip On The Buns

AT THE CLASS REUNION

Woman: It's been 30 years. Will you do that again?

FX: (doki doki) *Heartbeats—anticipation.*

Sensei: Nice buns. Any children...?

Woman: I've got two. I'm expecting a grandchild next year...

Commentary:

• This is another comic that brings upブルマ (buruma) and how disappointed a man can get by seeing it.

• You should take note of the blood spurting from the wife's nose after he slaps her. This is meant to show how extremely disappointed he is by seeing ブルマ (buruma) instead of her panties.

• Also please note, "Alice" is not just a simple English name to many Japanese, but instead, it carries the image of young, innocent girls in their early teens, like "Alice in Wonderland."

Commentary:

• 十八番 (juuhachiban) literally means number eighteen, but used in this context, it means some special (or unusual) action that defines a person. In this case, Sensei is remembered for his special method of punishing students, where he makes them lie on his lap while he slaps their behinds. His former students might not have liked his punishment at the time, but now they remember it fondly. In this comic strip, the author makes the point that even the most severe and disciplined Sensei can mellow with old age.

• Keep in mind that this comic strip depicts a world in which the concept of child molestation doesn't quite penetrate the general consciousness.

中学生

JUNIOR HIGH STUDENT

1—FX: (moji moji moji moji) *Timidly handing the magazine.*

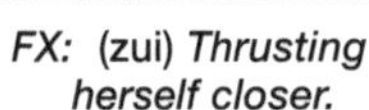

FX: (zui) *Thrusting herself closer.*

Sensei: Endo-kun, I heard you bought an Erohon yesterday.

Boy: Huh...? Sensei...

Boy: H—How did you find out?

Commentary:

- おめ (ome) is a colloquial pronunciation for the word おまえ (omae), which is used to address someone as "you" in a casual way.
- エロ本 (erohon)'s エロ (ero) is short for the English word "erotic" and 本 (hon) means book. エロ本 (erohon) means a magazine genre that generally appeals to the carnal desires of the male population, like "Playboy" or "Hustler."

お白洲

OSHIRASU

Magistrate: Chobei Bizenya

Bizenya: Yes, sir.

Magistrate: Capital crime!!

FX: (don) *A dramatic presentation*

Magistrate: Otsuta!!

Otsuta: ...Yes...

Magistrate: Live... well...

FX: (muki muki) Muscles bulging

Text: Muscle Magistrate—
The End

Commentary:

- お白州 (oshirasu) is a place inside a 奉行所 (bugyosho) where criminals are investigated. 奉行所 (bugyosho) is a public office where 奉行 (bugyo) works.
- 奉行 (bugyo), which is translated into magistrate, is a public official authorized to decide questions brought before a court of justice during 武家時代 (buke jidai = Buke Era, which encompasses the Kamakura Era through the Edo Era).
- The author is poking fun at the TV show called 遠山の金さん (Tooyama no Kinsan) which is a period piece with a 奉行 (bugyo) called 金さん (kinsan). At the end of each episode, 金さん (kinsan)'s trademark is to reveal his tattoo, which runs from his shoulder down to his upper arm.

大喜利

OOGIRI

Utamaru: High school girls of late, and—

Enraku: So, high school girls of late, and?

Utamaru: I say, the flower train of the strippers.

Enraku: And, the point is?

Utamaru: They allow you to watch but won't let you in.

Enraku: Ha ha ha. What was that? Take away all the cushions...

Enraku: ... So, the next question...

Utamaru: Uooooh.

Utamaru: Oooh.

おしおき♡

PUNISHMENT♥

Girl: In the name of the moon, I will punish you.

Men: Please punish me!

FX: (do do do do do) *A loud sound reminiscent of a stampede.*

Girl: Kyaa kyaa kyaa

Girl: In the name of the moon, I will punish you...

FX: (haa haa haa) *Breathing hard.*

Men: Please punish me!

FX: (do do do do do) *A loud sound reminiscent of a stampede.*

Girl: Kyaa kyaa kyaa kyaa

Commentary:

- 大喜利 (oogiri) refers to traditional Japanese comedy/humor, and that's what the popular TV show 笑点 (shoten) is all about. 笑点 (shoten) first appeared in 1966, and it has aired over 1,900 episodes. It continues to air every week, entertaining Japanese viewers.
- The likeness of 桂歌丸 (katsura utamaru) is on the right and 三遊亭遠楽 (sanyutei enraku) is on the left. If a joke is good, 遠楽 (enraku) hands out cushions, and if not, he asks that the cushions be taken away.
- The point of 歌丸 (utamaru)'s joke is that high school girls are the same as the flower train of the strippers, in that both of them will let you watch but won't let you in (i.e. the girls won't let you have sex with them, and you can't ride on the flower train).

Commentary:

- This comic strip is making fun of a popular Japanese anime called "Sailor Moon." In the anime, a heroic girl who wears セーラー服 (sēlā fuku) fights against evil.
- Also please note that she's wearing a typical school uniform called セーラー服 (sēlā fuku). This is a typical uniform for junior high and high school girls.
- Although おしおき (oshioki) literally means "punishment," it is sometimes used to mean "giving sexual stimulation." That's why, in this comic strip, men are rushing to be punished by the girl.
- The ironic twist is that it looks more like the girl is being punished than the men.

シリーズ ひとコマ番外地(ばんがいち)

Series Irregular One Panel Page

雪国(ゆきぐに)の定番(ていばん)

It's always the case in the snow country.

ボンタンに長(なが)ぐつ

Bontans and boots.

Boy: No matter how I try, I can't look cool in this.

Commentary:

• ぼんたん (bontan) is a super-baggy-style pants worn as a school uniform for boys. ぼんたん (bontan) style is particularly favored by delinquent students, who consider it to be very cool to wear. It's just that, the snow boots don't go with ぼんたん (bontan)...

• Here is a picture of ぼんたん (bontan) style pants worn as a school uniform:

ケンちゃん

KEN-CHAN

Mother: Ken-chan, it's about time you come out.

Mother: Kazu-kun has made an effort to come over so that you can make up...

FX: (su) *Swiftly and quietly.*

Mother: Geez. You're really shy, aren't you...?

Commentary:

- There was a TV series that first started in 1968 with ケンちゃん (ken-chan) as the main character. The ケンちゃん (ken-chan) in that series was a shy boy, and the readers who remember the series may read this comic strip with a sense of nostalgia.
- To understand the word 恥ずかしがり屋さん (hazukashi-gari-yasan), it's best to break it into smaller pieces. 恥ずかしい (hazukashii) means being shy, while 恥ずかしがり (hazukashigari) means the characteristic of being shy. 屋さん (yasan) is used to typify a person being one way or the other. So, in this case, 恥ずかしがり屋さん (hazukashi-gari-yasan) means a person who is very shy.
- Here are a couple of variations to the word with 屋さん (yasan): 泣き虫屋さん (nakimushi-yasan = a person who easily cries), 食いしん坊屋さん (kuishinbo-yasan = a person who likes to eat a lot).

金魚 (きんぎょ) — GOLDFISH

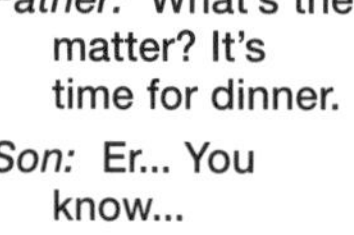

Father: What's the matter? It's time for dinner.

Son: Er... You know...

Son: They were a pair, so I feel bad about it...

Father: Let's hurry and eat...

Son: Yeah.

Commentary:

• つがい (tsugai) means a pair, like a husband and wife, or a male and a female. Apparently, they cooked one of them.

• From panel #3 and #4, it appears that Father and Son live in a small place with a 畳 (tatami = straw mat) flooring. Without much else to eat that day, the goldfish was tempting enough for them to cook, despite...

都庁物語 (とちょうものがたり) — STORY OF CAPITAL CITY

FX: (buwa) *Flare up.*

Girl: Oh no, a wind tunnel between the buildings!

FX: (hyooo) *A whistling sound made by the blowing wind.*

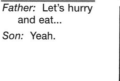

FX: (ooooo) *An extension of the FX from panel #2.*

FX: (ooooo) *An extension of the FX from panel #2 and #3.*

Text: The End

Commentary:

• In a city like Tokyo, a windy gap between two buildings can be a big nuisance.

• Here is a picture showing the typical forest of buildings in Toyko, where wind corridors are often created:

誕生日 (たんじょうび)

BIRTHDAY

Radio: Greeting from Hiroshi Tamaoki with a smile!!

Detective: It's coming up.

Radio: It's time for the "Congratulation Corner." Today, an investigating detective from Tama

Radio: sends his congratulations for the 54th birthday of Masakichi Shigeno, a suspect.

FX: (pachi pachi pachi) *Clapping hands.*

Shigeno: I killed Endo, Mr. Detective...

Detective: You've understood, haven't you?

Commentary:

• Hiroshi Tamaoki is a widely known radio talk show host and TV announcer. The radio program called 玉置宏の笑顔でこんにちは (Tamaoki Hiroshi no egaode konnichiwa), which translates to "Greeting from Hiroshi Tamaoki with a smile," was actually on air from 1978 to 1996. おめでとうコーナー (omedetou kounaa), which translates to "Congratulations Corner," was part of the program. Because of it, this comic strip has special meaning to Japanese readers who are familiar with the show.

• In panel #4, the Detective says わかってくれたか (wakatte kuretaka), which, in itself, means "you've understood, haven't you?" However, what is unsaid but implied is "I'm glad you've understood my goodwill."

チュー♡

CHU♥

FX: (chu...) *Smooch...*

FX: (chu... chu...) *Smooch... smooch...*

FX: (chuchu chu chuchu) *Smack, smooch, smack.*

Boy: Hmm... You've got a lot more pimples than I expected...

FX: *(zee zee) Breathing hard, as if choking or feeling ill.*

Girl: I'm so sorry.

Commentary:

• The couple appears to be either in junior high or high school. This is apparent by the typical school uniform that the boy is wearing.

• Here is a picture of a typical school uniform that boys tend to wear in Japan:

大丈夫ですか?

ARE YOU ALRIGHT?

Man 1: Are yah alright...?

Girl: S'okay. Go 'way.

Man 2: He's buggin' her.

Man 2: Are yah alright?

Man 1: Are yah alright?

Girl: Okay, I said! Okay!

Commentary:

• They're all drunk, and the girl is puking.

• The drunken men tried to say 大丈夫ですか (daijobu desuka) which means "are you alright?" However, they could not pronounce the sentence properly and ended up saying 大丈夫れすかぁ (daijobu resukaa). Please note, the girl could not say 大丈夫です (daijobu desu = I'm okay) properly either, and that's why we know she's just as drunk as the men.

散歩

A STROLL

FX: (totete tetetete) *Quick, light footsteps.*

Dog: Ruff ruff♥

Man: How fast you are! Ho ho ho ho

FX: (burororo...) *Vroom.*

Dog: Ruff ruff ruff♥

FX: (totetetete) *Quick, light footsteps.*

FX: (buroroooh) *Vroom vroom.*

Man: How fast you are! Ho ho hohoho

Dog: Ruff ruff♥

Man: How fast you are! Ho ho ho

FX: (buroroooh) *Vroom vroom.*

Commentary:

- It's supposed to be a stroll!
- The author is poking fun at modern pet owners.

クレーン

CRANE

FX: (pa pa raah) *Honking car.*

FX: (buroro...) *Vroom.*

FX: (buroro) *Vroom.*

FX: (pa rara) *Honking car.*

Worker: Howdy. I'm the operator of this crane...

FX: (uzu uzu) *Itching to drop.*

Worker: I wish I could drop an iron bar down—just for once...

FX: (pa pa raah) *Honking car.*

FX: (buroro...) *Vroom.*

FX: (buroro) *Vroom.*

FX: (pa rara) *Honking car.*

Commentary:

- うずうず (uzu uzu) is an expression indicating that a person is itching or dying to do something. In this case, the crane operator, who is tormented by the loud, obnoxious traffic, dreams of dropping an iron bar down to silence the traffic. Just imagine what the author saw when he noticed a large construction site in the middle of the city with an enormous crane precariously perched high above.

ごめんね

SO SORRY

Boy: Dammit, it's too hard to slice with this knife.

Senpai: You're doing it wrong. Let me show you how...

Senpai: Slice between the bones.

FX: (saku) *An easy and soft feel.*

Senpai: That's how you get a clean slice.

Boy: Wow. You're right. The knife slices easily.

Senpai: Ha ha ha...

Senpai: Don't forget this technique, okay?

Boy: I'm so sorry, Senpai...

Commentary:

• From panel #4, it's obvious that the boy is a member of the Yakuza. It's the Yakuza's tradition to punish blunders by cutting off the culprit's pinky. Two men standing by the boy are Yakuza, watching how the boy would perform and bear the punishment. Remembering the technique taught by his Senpai, the boy regrets how he must use it to cut off his own pinky. He is aware that the Senpai would have never expected that this technique would become useful in such a way.

にちようび 日曜日

SUNDAY

Girl 1: It's best to relax on Sundays.

Girl 2: Let's try doing something different and fun.

Girl 2: Hey! Let's go! Ho ho ho

FX: (gororo... goro goro goro goro) *Rolling down.*

Girl 1: Hoh ho ho ho

FX: (goro goro goro goro goro goro) Rolling down.

FX: (gero gero gero gero... gero gero gero gero) Vomiting hard.

Commentary:

• ホホホ (ho ho ho) is a high-pitched, feminine laugh.

• ゴロゴロ (goro goro) is a rumbling sort of sound indicative of a rolling object.

• ゲロ (gero) is the derogatory use of a word 反吐 (hedo) which is equivalent to the word vomit. When the word ゲロ (gero) is repeated, it expresses the intensity of the vomiting. ゲロゲロ (gero gero) is also recognized as a croaky sort of sound.

• It was supposed to be a relaxing Sunday...

あーん♡

AHN♥

3個ちょうだい

たこ焼

Customer 1: Three of them please.

Text: Takoyaki

Woman: Three here. Please open up your mouth♥ Ahn.

Customer 2: Oneh-san... three for me too. Hee hee hee...

Woman: 250 yen please.

Customer 2: She won't do it to me.

Commentary:

• あーん (ahn) is a vocal sound often made by a person when he/she wants someone else to open his/her mouth wide, like in a dentist's office.

• たこ焼 (takoyaki) is a type of snack food that is usually served at street stands. The shape and size are like a golf ball, and its ingredients include octopus. That's why たこ焼 (takoyaki) is sometimes referred to as octopus balls in English.

• Here is a picture of a typical Takoyaki and Takoyaki stand:

海岸

BEACH

FX: (zazaan zazaan) *Breaking waves.*

Girl: Sensei♥

FX: (basha basha) *Splashing sound.*

FX: (zazaan zazaan) *Breaking waves.*

Sensei: Don't wear shorts!!!

FX: (ban) Bang.

Commentary:

• The image of a girl running towards a man 先生 (sensei) on a beach when the sun is setting is a cliché found in many Japanese 青春 (seishun) melodramas.

• Now, you can see how the author has twisted this melodramatic cliché into a gag by adding theブルマ (buruma) humor at the end.

SPRING

FX: (sawa sawa sawa) *A pleasant wind blowing.*

FX: (ba) *A dramatic moment.*

FX: (ta ta ta) *Quickly rushing away.*

Boy: Is this what they call first love...?

FX: (doki doki doki doki) *Throbbing heart.*

Commentary:

• ドキドキ (doki doki) indicates that a person's heart is throbbing noticeably.

• 初恋 (hatsukoi) means first love, or falling in love for the first time. The idea of 初恋 (hatsukoi) also brings to mind how a person's heart throbs in a ドキドキ (doki doki) way.

• What's funny about this comic strip is that the adolescent boy saw the girl's panties, which gets his heart throbbing with excitement. However, the boy starts to think he's falling in love, just because he felt so ドキドキ (doki doki).

シリーズ
ひとコマ番外地

① 満員電車にて

② きたないけど
ぬいてみたい…

③ ゴトトン

ゴトトン

④ ウズ
ウズ

Series
Irregular One Panel Page

① Text: Inside the packed train.

② Girl: It's yucky, but I want to pull it...

③ FX: (gototon gototon) The rattling sound of the moving train.

④ FX: (uzu uzu) Itching to pull the hair out.

Commentary:

• 満員電車 (manin densha) is something Japanese commuters experience on a daily basis—especially those who live in big cities like Tokyo. Being packed so tightly together often forces a person to notice something he/she would never have noticed otherwise.

• Here is a typical 満員電車 (manin densha):

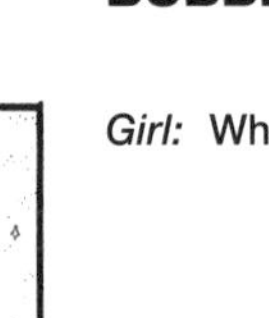

BUBBLES

Girl: Whoaah

FX: *(suu) A sucking sound.*

Girl: Don't swallow...

FX: *(suu) A sucking sound.*

Commentary:

• Place yourself in the position of the little girl, and maybe you can see what the little girl felt like when a very, very, very old woman did that to her bubbles.

• Now place yourself in the position of the old woman, and breath deeply. Only then, perhaps you can taste the bubble and feel how refreshing it is to suck in something so young and vibrant, or have a bad taste in your mouth. You decide which it is.

JUDO CLUB

Man 1: Er—

Man 2: ?

Man 2: What's up with him?

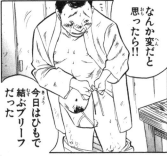

Man 1: I knew something was odd!!

Man 1: Today, I'm wearing underwear that needs to be tied on.

Man 2: Don't wear that weird stuff!!!

Commentary:

• The underwear that he's wearing is not traditional underwear for men. For many Japanese readers, his skimpy underwear is likely to appear bizarre, especially when it's worn by someone like a Judo player. It's like a macho man wearing woman's bikini.

コインランドリー

COIN LAUNDRY

FX: (goun goun gouun goun) *The dull sound of the laundry machine going.*

FX: (soro soro soro) *Quietly sneak in.*

FX: (goun goun goun goun) *The dull sound of the laundry machine going.*

Song: Oh, the field is full of green grass...

FX: (biku) *Startled or alarmed.*

Man: How 'bout singing togeth-er until the laundry gets dried?

Boy: No, thanks...

Commentary:

• おー牧場は緑 (oh makiba wa midori) is a classic folksong from The Czech Republic. What gives this comic strip an edge is the fact that the rough-looking man is not only fully naked while doing his laundry, but he begins singing this classic song—which any kid could sing. To top it off, he invites the frightened young man to join in and sing. Perhaps he's not as scary as he appears...

ももレンジャー

PINK RANGER

Monster: Pink Ranger, this is it!!

Ranger: Kuuu

Ranger: Uryaa

Ranger: Toryaah

Monster: Don't wear shorts! And take this (job more) seri-ously.

FX: [poke] *The sound of the slap/punch.*

Commentary:

• Obviously, this ももレンジャー (momo renjaa) series is playing off the well-known TV show "*Power Rangers.*"

• くううッ (kuuu) is a gasp, indicating that the person is in the tight spot.

•うりゃあっ (uryaa) and とりゃあっ (toryaah) are forceful Kiai-like shouts of concentration.

• The monsters are all acted by men, and yet again, the author is poking fun at how men simply can't stand ブルマ (buruma).

スケスケ教師

SEE-THROUGH TEACHER

Text: "Kyaa, is someone there!?" The See-Through Teacher was terrified.

There was a shadow right behind her!!

Text: "No!! Please don't!!"

A mysterious man assaulted See-Through Teacher!!

Text: "Sensei, it's me." It was her student, Taguchi-kun.

"I was only trying to scare you."

"Oh, was that all?"

The two of them laughed cheerfully.

—- The End.

Boy 1: These old plastic covered magazines!!

Boy 2: I don't know, but they were pretty hip.

Commentary:

• ビニ本 (bini hon) was a plastic covered magazine sold through vending machines in 1970s. The genre of magazine is currently called エロ本 (erohon), and they are now sold without the plastic cover. Unlike ビニ本 (bini hon), エロ本 (erohon) is not sold through vending machines, and even if you find the old vending machines that look like the ones which could sell ビニ本 (bini hon), they're probably not operational.

泣きの高橋

CRYBABY TAKAHASHI

Song: You and I fought in the army together...

Takahashi: Uwaaaaan!

Man: Looks like Crybaby Takahashi's making his appearance.

Man: You're always like that as soon as you get drunk.

Takahashi: The lyrics for this song are so sad—too sad!!

Takahashi: This line here's also very sad!!

Man: C'mon now...

Commentary:

• うわああああん (uwaaaaan) is the vocal sound of a person crying out loud.

• It's not uncommon to see a grown man crying at a party after he gets completely drunk. There is a word that describes someone like that, which reads 泣き上戸 (naki jogo). 泣き (naki) is an adjective of 泣く(naku), which means "to cry." 上戸 (jogo) means someone who drinks a lot of alcohol. When the adjective 泣き (naki) is attached to the word 上戸 (jogo), the meaning of the word 上戸 (jogo) changes to signify this unique behavioral tendency after getting drunk. So, 泣き上戸 (naki jogo) means someone who starts crying once he/she gets drunk. Another variation is 笑い上戸 (warai jogo), which means someone who gets jolly once he/she gets drunk.

• In this comic strip, the author is depicting a typical 泣き上戸 (naki jogo) embodied in the behavior exhibited by 高橋 (takahashi).

筋肉奉行2

MUSCLE MAGISTRATE 2

Magistrate: I shall not deprive you of seeing my muscles.

Criminal 1: What? It can't be!!

Woman: Arrgh

Criminal 2: You, just give up!

Criminal 1: You're so evil...

Criminal 2: Ho ho ho...

FX: *(gaan) An expression indicating that they're stunned and feel as if rocks are being dropped onto their heads.*

Criminal 1: You're that body builder who's passed us by!!!

Magistrate: Confess!!

Commentary:

• ボディビルダー (bodibirudaa) is the English word "bodybuilder." This word was definitely not in general use during 武家時代 (buke jidai = Buke Era, which encompasses the Kamakura Era through the Edo Era).

• This is another one of the Muscle Magistrate series in which the author is poking fun at the TV show 遠山の金さん (Tooyama no Kinsan).

姉妹坂

SHIMAIZAKA

Sister 1: Thiiiiis

Sister 1: is how small you were when

Sister 1: I, the Aunty, first got to know you, you know.

FX: (pa kaaan) *The high-pitched sound of a smack.*

Text: THE END

Commentary:

• 姉妹坂 (shimaizaka) is the title of a manga series by Kazue Ohyama. This series first appeared in 1979. 姉妹 (shimai) means sisters, and 坂 (saka) means a slope. It's about four sisters, their youth, and their loves. It depicts how they persevere, despite a series of misfortunes that befall them. The manga series was made into movie in 1985.

• If you keep this fact in mind and read between the lines, you'll begin to see the twist the author made in the sisters' relationship, and how the little girl may relate to them.

再婚 RE-MARRIAGE

Daughter: What is it?

Daughter: What's going on, Dad?

Father: As a matter of fact,

Father: I'm thinking of getting married again...

Daughter: If that's something you've already thought about carefully, I can't say anything against it.

Daughter: It's your life after all.

Father: Alright then.

Father: Let me introduce her. She's our neighbor Moko-chan.

Moko: How do'y do.

Commentary:

• よろちく (yorochiku) is a baby talk version of よろしく (yoroshiku). This indicates that Moko is a very young girl whose spoken language skills are still developing.

• よろしく (yoroshiku) is a common Japanese phrase used to solicit good will and favors. In this case, it's said as a form of greeting.

はぢらい BASHFULNESS

FX: (fuwaa) *Lightly blowing up by the wind*

Girl: Kyaa.

Girl: Oh no...

FX: (kaaah) *Blush.*

Girl: That's it♥

Men: Ooh.

FX: (pachi pachi) *Clapping hands.*

Man 1: In terms of bashfulness, she is the best...

Man 2: She's made it difficult for the other challengers...

Man 3: Next person please...

Commentary:

• はぢらい (hajirai) or 恥じらい (hajirai) is a feeling that makes people blush due to shyness, bashfulness or naiveté. Not only middle-aged men, but Japanese males in general tend to find it attractive when a female possesses the quality of 恥じらい (hajirai).

• In this comic strip, the author captures the Japanese men's sensitivity by showing the way in which 恥じらい (hajirai) is expressed can make a difference in winning men's approval.

下町の太陽

THE SUN OF THE DOWN-TOWN

Young man: Downtown's really nice.

FX: (da) *Dashing away.*

Tora-san: Ah uhhh...

Tora-san: Farewell, Sakura.

Sakura: Wait! Bro!!

FX: (ta ta ta ta) *Rushing after the man.*

Man: Please wait a minute, bro.

Young man: What tranquil scenery...

FX: (jiiin) *Impressed or touched.*

馬

STUD

Girl: What a big horse!

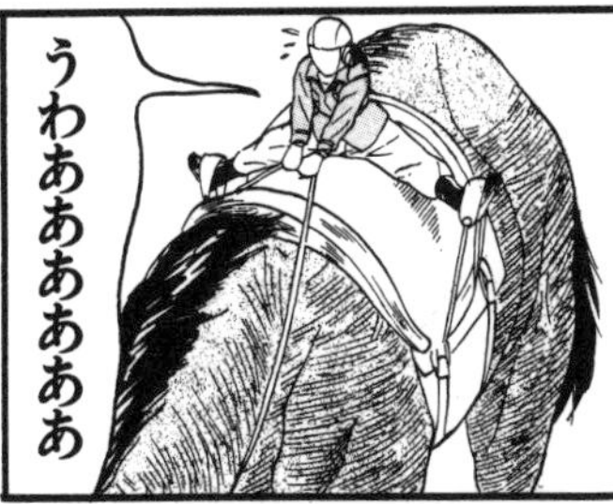

Girl: Uwaaaaaaa *(Whoaaaa!)*

FX: (bako bako bako) *A loud galloping sound.*

Girl: Gyaaaaah!

Girl: Gyaaaaah!

FX: (bako bako bako) *A loud galloping sound.*

Commentary:

• The character illustrated in panel #2 is the likeness of 寅さん (Tora-san), who is the famous downtown Tokyo character in the movie series called 男はつらいよ (otokowa tsuraiyo). 男 (otoko) means man, and つらいよ (tsurai) means hard, painful, trying or bitter. So, the title can be translated to read "It's tough to be a man." The series started in 1969 and continued through 1996, with 48 episodes.

• サクラ (sakura) is 寅さん (Tora-san)'s sister, and the man that appears in panel #4 is her husband. お義兄さん (onii-san) there means brother-in-law.

• 寅さん (Tora-san) is regarded as someone who encapsulates the heart of Japanese sensitivity and is loved by all. That's why the title reads "the sun of the downtown," meaning 寅さん (Tora-san) is the sun.

• The twist is, the young man does not recognize the dramatic event that's taking place, but instead, simply revels in the idea of 寅さん (Tora-san), as well as the downtown itself.

Commentary:

• うわあああああああ (uwaaaaaaa) is an exclamation that indicates surprise and sometimes admiration.

• ぎゃああああああ (gyaaaaaa) is a shriek of pain.

• Use your imagination, and you'll know why this comic strip could either make you laugh or feel uncomfortable.

屋上の詩 LYRIC OF THE ROOFTOP

Man: What an uneventful place the department store's rooftop is during the weekday...!

FX: (poka poka poka) *Cozy, warm sunshine.*

FX: (utsura utsura) *Dozing.*

FX: (poka poka) Cozy, warm sunshine.

Man: A housewife is taking a nap over there.

Man: And a girl is being bullied over there.

FX: (poka poka) *Cozy, warm sunshine.*

Man: And an adult video is being filmed without a permission....

FX: (poka poka poka) *Cozy, warm sunshine.*

英語教師 ENGLISH TEACHER

FX: (puri puri) *Sexy hip swing.*

FX: (puri puri puri) *Sexy hip swing.*

FX: (kuru) *Spin around.*

FX: (sa) *Quick move.*

Student 1: Wakame-chan's become an English teacher!

Student 2: Don't know what's going on, but I'm glad.

Commentary:

• In Tokyo, as well as in other big Japanese cities, a lot of department stores have 屋上 (okujo), which is a rooftop area used by the public as a park. Like typical parks in big cities around the world, various people gather there and go about their own activities.

• Here's a picture of a typical 屋上 (okujo) on top of a department store:

Commentary:

• As mentioned earlier, ワカメちゃん (Wakame-chan) is a well-known anime character from the anime series called "サザエさん" (Sazae-san). In the anime, she's a perpetual nine-year-old with her trademark haircut and mini-skirt with her panties showing.

• In this comic, the author has brought back ワカメちゃん (Wakame-chan) in another setting, where she is now a sexy English teacher, with her trademark haircut and mini-skirt with her panties showing. Many Japanese readers, who grew up with the series, will find it very funny to see ワカメちゃん (Wakame-chan) as a grown woman in this context.

シリーズ

かわしまにっき
川島日記

Series
Kawashima's Diary

野宿(のじゅく)は
やっぱ
10月(がつ)までだネ

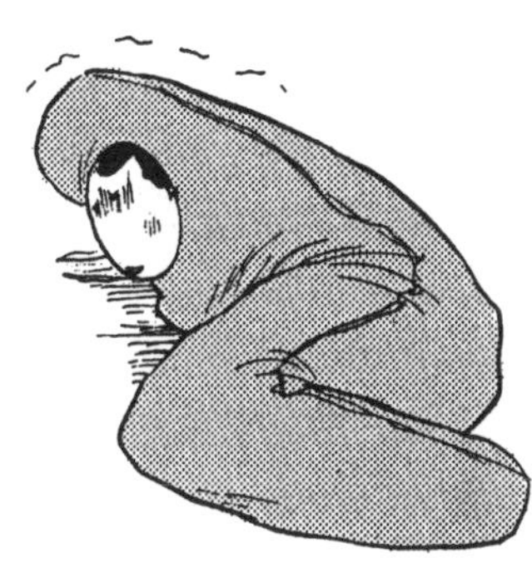

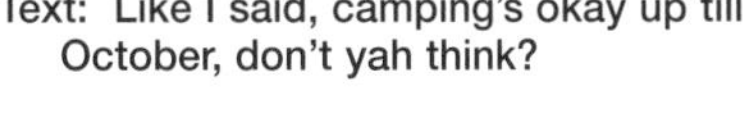

Text: Like I said, camping's okay up till October, don't yah think?

Commentary:

• Here the author is making fun of camping at the wrong time of year. It's simply not worth freezing inside a sleeping bag at night. If you don't have the proper equipment, you'd better stick to camping in the summer.

つうきんでんしゃ 通勤電車 COMMUTER TRAIN

Girls: (kya ha ha) *Giggling.*

Girls: (ha ha ha...) *Laughter.*

FX: (goton goton) *The rattling sound of the moving train.*

Girls: (kya ha ha) *Giggling.*

Girls: (ha ha ha...) *Laughter.*

FX: (gototon goton... goto-ton... goton) *The rattling sound of the moving train.*

Man: You can't call yourself a pro unless you can stop right before it shows...

Man: Here's pay-ment for your work today...

Girl: Yes, I under-stand. Sorry about that.

Commentary:

• Since the girls are wearing school uniforms, they're probably high school students.

• バイト (baito) means "part-time job". From the uniform he's wearing, readers can see that the man handing over the money is one of the train-station employees.

• This is a typical version of the so-called "nonsense gag" or "absurd manga." The reader is left wondering what exactly it's supposed to mean. I have a hunch, but I'll let you decide for yourself. Just remember that this author likes to depict middle-aged men obsessed with high school girls.

そうまとう 走馬燈 KALEIDO-SCOPE

Man: Am I going to die...?

Text: Events from the past are appearing like a kaleidoscopic images....

Man: Who's she...? I don't know her...

Man: Ug ugh...

Man: Ug ugh...

Commentary:

• 走馬灯 (sōmatō) is a revolving lantern. There's a saying in Japanese that a dying person sees a series of kaleidoscopic images from his/her past like the shadows cast by a revolving lantern.

• This dying man is seeing images, but somehow, he is not seeing anyone he knows from his past.

• This can simply be interpreted as something funny to laugh at, or it can have a deeper meaning, like, perhaps, the man had a previous life in which he knew those people.

ももレンジャー2

PINK RANGER 2

Ranger: What's up? Why aren't you attacking me?

Ranger: What? This? I picked culottes...

Ranger: It's easier to move, you know....

Ranger: Wh— What's so wrong about it?

ウニの物語

STORY OF SEA URCHIN

②—*FX:* (chobi) *A tiny bit.*

③—*FX:* (sesse) *Working hard and diligently.*

Customer: Hyaaah, delicious!! It's out of this world.

Customer: Another one please.

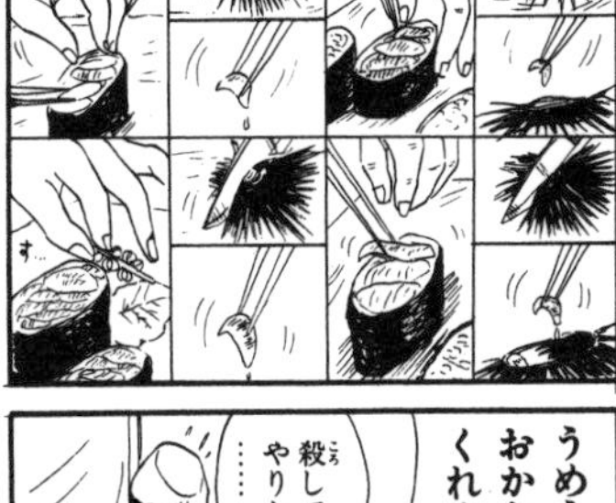

FX: (su) *Swiftly and gently.*

Customer: Delicious!! Another one please.

Sushi Chef: I wanna kill him...

Commentary:

• As mentioned earlier, this ももレンジャー (momo renjaa) series is the spin on the well-known TV show "*Power Rangers.*"

• In the 1960s, at the same time the culottes-style skirt became fashionable in Western Society, it appeared in Japan. In this comic strip, the author is making fun of men's desire to catch a glimpse of women's panties, as well as the impact the culottes-style skirt had on popular culture.

Commentary:

• ウニ (uni) or sea urchin is a spiny, hard-shelled sea creature, whose fresh roe is considered a delicacy. You can find it at most sushi bars in Japan, as well as the United States. With their spiny shells protecting their roe, sea urchins require skillful handling and concentration to prepare. It also requires several sea urchins before enough fresh roe is collected for a single order of sushi. You can imagine how the Sushi Chef felt when the customer gobbled up the sushi in an instant, after he toiled so hard to prepare it.

• Here is a picture of ウニ (uni) and how it is typically served in a sushi bar:

ぽてっ

POTE

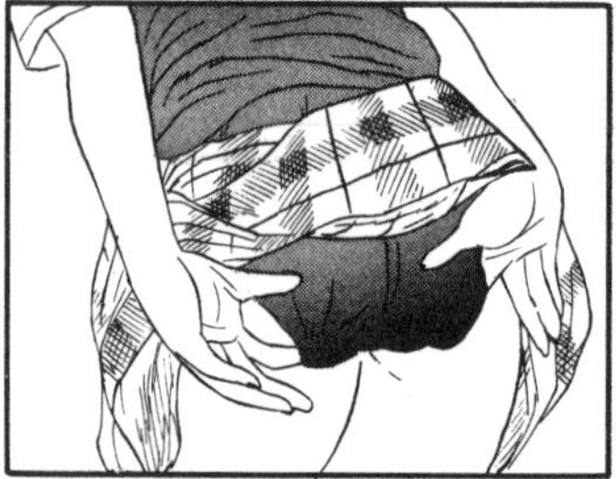

FX: (pote) *Smack.*

Men: Ooooh

FX: (pachi pachi pachi pachi pachi) *Clapping hands.*

Man 1: Her "Buruma Pote Pote" is the best!!

Man 2: I—I agree!!

Commentary:

• Smacking the edges of ブルマ (buruma) is a behavior that occurs when a female who wears ブルマ (buruma) wants to check to make sure that her panties are not sticking out or when she needs to adjust the way it fits.

• If you thought how silly these men are and laughed, you got the joke. Although it might be viewed as kinky, some Japanese men find it exciting to see young girls stick their fingers in like that. And, of course, the author has exaggerated the point.

せんぱい 先輩

SENPAI

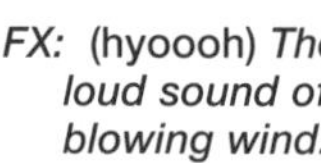

FX: (hyoooh) *The loud sound of blowing wind.*

FX: (huasaa) *Gently.*

Boy: Senpai♥

Senpai: Hmm...

Text: The End

Commentary:

• Unlike Western Society, where certain religious beliefs forbid homosexuality, being gay in Japan is not as frowned upon as you might imagine. Most people aren't dogmatically for or against it.

• On the other hand, the fact that being gay is determined primarily by a person's biology, not choice, is a concept that hasn't quite permeated Japanese society yet. This is partly because most people in Japan believe being gay is a life-style choice made by artists, movies stars and other celebrities. Many Japanese tend to assume these are a special breed of people, who allow themselves to act in this way. Thus, it's more or less accepted within this context, especially in a large, metropolitan areas, like Tokyo.

• Most Japanese have the stereotypical image of gay men as pretty and feminine looking young guys. Otherwise, it would seem too weird. What's interesting about this comic strip is the fact that the author is portraying two gay boys, who look like "the boys-next-door," no different than anyone else.

改札

TICKET GATE

FX: *(kachi kachi kachi kachi kachi) Click, click, click, click, click.*

FX: *(zawa zawa) Unintelligible noise of the crowd.*

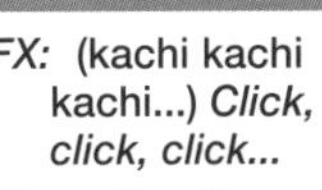

FX: *(kachi kachi kachi...) Click, click, click...*

Man: Sir, what are you counting?

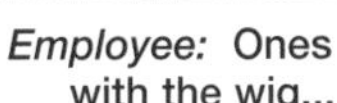

Employee: Ones with the wig...

FX: *(kachi kachi kachi kachi kachi kachi) Click, click, click, click, click, click.*

FX: *(kachi kachi kachi kachi kachi...) Click, click, click, click, click, click, click...*

飯場の花2

FLOWER OF THE CONSTRUCTION CAMP 2

Song: A nurse in the countryside is riding on a...

Song: La la la la, passionate Mariko is on fire...

Girl: I'm going now♥ See you tomorrow at the site.

Man: ...Yup, see you tomorrow...

Commentary:

• 駅員 (eki-in) is a person who works at the train station. ヅラ (zura) is a derogatory term for wig.

• I don't know how this 駅員 (eki-in) can tell who's wearing a wig. That said, the social commentary in this comic strip will make many Japanese readers laugh, that is, if they don't feel too uncomfortable.

• Here's a picture of typical ticket gate in Tokyo during rush hour:

Commentary:

• I wonder what it would be like if this same situation occurred in America. Would male construction workers remain as passive as they are depicted here? I doubt it.

• You might also find it interesting that this comic depicts mellow Japanese construction workers watching a girl behave in a way that seems a bit absurd.

スケスケ先生

SEE-THROUGH TEACHER

Teacher: Why aren't any of you friendly to me?

Teacher: Is that because I'm the See-Through Teacher...?

Teacher: Is that because you can see through me?

Student 1: That's not true.

Student 2: We love you the way you are.

Teacher: So you say, but you still keep your distance...

FX: (moji moji moji moji moji) Squirming shyly.

Commentary:

• Most heterosexual men find it exciting to see a woman naked—but not quite fully. Since Japanese media is forbidden from showing male or female genitalia, due to government censorship, most Japanese men use their imagination to fill in the blanks. In some ways, the power of the imagination can excite men's sexuality more than actually seeing everything.

• Given this, you can see how the See-Through Teacher is the embodiment of the young, male students' fantasy. The twist is in the universal difference between men and women. Although the male instinct makes the boys want to reach out and touch her, their inhibitions stop them—while the female teacher doesn't seem to understand their psychology and feels rejected.

シリーズ
川島日記
1985の川島
朝日連峰に
のぼった記念に
山頂に堀ちえみの
ラミネートカードを
埋めた

Series
Kawashima's Diary

Kawashima in 1985—To memorialize the climbing of the Asahi Mountain Range, I buried the laminated card of Chiemi Hori.

Commentary:

• 掘りちえみ (Hori Chiemi) was one of the top idols of the 1980s. She made her first debut in 1982 and her most successful role was in the TV drama series スチュワーデス物語 (suchuwaadesu monogatari = A Story of a Stewardess).

• This diary reveals yet another of the author's many eccentricities.

スケスケ先生 未踏峰

SEE-THROUGH TEACHER, UNTRODDEN MOUNTAIN

FX: *(baaaah) Dramatically falling.*

Fukami: See-Through Teacher!!

Boy: Whoaaaa!

Teacher: F—Fukami-kun!!

FX: (baaaah) *Dramatically showing.*

FX: (baaaah) *Dramatically falling.*

Fukami: L—Lord Almighty!! Is this the reward?

Fukami: The price is too high, dammit!!

Commentary:

• Let's examine the boy's family name, 深見 (fukami). The Kanji character 深 (fuka) means deep, and 見 (mi) means watch. So, his name is Mr. Deep Watch.

• The author's obsession with men's desire to glimpse female panties is given a twist in this comic strip: even Mr. Deep Watch thinks it isn't worth the trouble to see her panties in exchange for falling off a cliff. The point being that even a man's fetish for female panties has its limits. The irony is that the See-Through Teacher's skirt does not need to be lifted for anyone to see her panties.

いやな男

LOATHSOME MAN

Woman: I say Naoto Ogata is cute after all♥.

Man: Humph!! He's a kid, just a kid...

Woman: Can't stop thinking about Masatoshi Nagase of late...

Man: Urrgh, I wouldn't want to get laid by him.

Woman: But, Ken Takakura looks young no matter what...

Man: Ken-san...♥

Woman: Don't you dare comment on every-thing!!

FX: (dokah) *A loud and a strong kick.*

Commentary:

• 緒方なおと (ogata naoto) is a round, baby-faced actor. 永瀬正敏 (nagaze masatoshi) is a hip and slick actor. 高倉健 (takakura ken) is an old actor who first debuted in the 1950s. He went on to launch an international career in films like Black Rain and Mr. Baseball (1990). Over the years, he has appeared in more than 200 films.

• Unlike the younger actors, 高倉健 (takakura ken) is loved by many middle-aged men, due to his persona that embodies 義理 (giri) and 人情 (ninjo). 義理 (giri) is a sense of justice, duty, obligation and honor. 人情 (ninjo) is the emotion which makes us human.

• Instead of "three strikes and you're out," she took the initiative and prevented his annoying comment—except that we already know what he thought.

おうだん ほどう
横断歩道のメルヘン

CROSSWALK FAIRY TALE

Girl: Let's go across together, Obah-chan.

Old Woman: Thank you...

Girl: Good bye, Obah-chan.

Old Woman: I don't know who you are, but thank you.

Text: In fact, this old woman was...

Text: Isuzu Yamada, but...

Text: The girl lived the rest of her life without knowing that fact.

Commentary:

• 山田五十鈴 (yamada isuzu) is a famous actress who appeared in over 100 movies. Born in 1917, she began her acting career at age 12. The first movie she appeared in was made in 1930. She has married six times and has captured the media's attention throughout most of her active career.

• After all, even the most celebrated actress eventually becomes old, and by then, the media attention is pretty much non-existent. Even 山田五十鈴 (yamada isuzu) can walk around town without a stranger noticing who she is...

• And, yes, no one can beat the beauty of youth...

めし

DINNER

Husband: Who can eat this horrible dinner?!!

Sachiko: (buhe) *About to burst out crying.*

FX: *(koro koro) Rolling away.*

Husband: (zee zee zee) *Breathing heavily.*

Sachiko: (waa waa) *Crying out loud.*

Sachiko: (waaaa) *Crying louder.*

Sachiko: (waaaaaaa) *Crying even louder.*

Husband: I'm sorry, Sachiko...

Text: Child Bride—The End

Commentary:

• As you become familiar with the Gloom Party series, you'll realize that おさな妻 (osanazuma) turns into a series within Gloom Party, depicting the continuing drama of Sachiko, the pre-K girl. Oddly enough, she is the wife of an irresponsible grown man. 幼い (osanai) means infant, juvenile, childish or immature, and 妻 (tsuma) means wife. This Sachiko series, a.k.a., Sacchan series, is considered by many readers the highlight of Gloom Party, and once they're hooked, they like to keep reading to find out what happens next.

• Please note, there's a movie called おさな妻 (osanazuma) that was released in 1970. It was a big hit, and the title おさな妻 (osanazuma), which refers to girls who were married in their teens, became a popular pronoun at the time.

そくりょう
測量 SURVEY

マンホール中心にあわせてね

Man: Will you place it right in the center of the manhole?

Girl: Like this?

Man: That's perfect.

電信柱いってみようか…

Man: Let's do that telephone pole...

Girl: Like this?

Man: That's perfect.

Commentary:

• Here's another version of the comic strip depicting men's fetish over female panties. The author portrays in a comical way how a serious-looking man at work can be thinking of something else besides the work at hand.

• Obviously, the girl is oblivious to what's going on in the man's mind—and that's what makes it so thrilling and humorous.

たなきゅうこう
棚急行 SHELF EXPRESS

このぶんだと会議に間にあわないな
ゴトトン
ゴトトン…
ぶ部長ォ…

Bucho: At this rate, we won't make it to the conference.

FX: (gototon goton...) *The rattling sound of the moving train.*

Subordinate: B—Bucho...

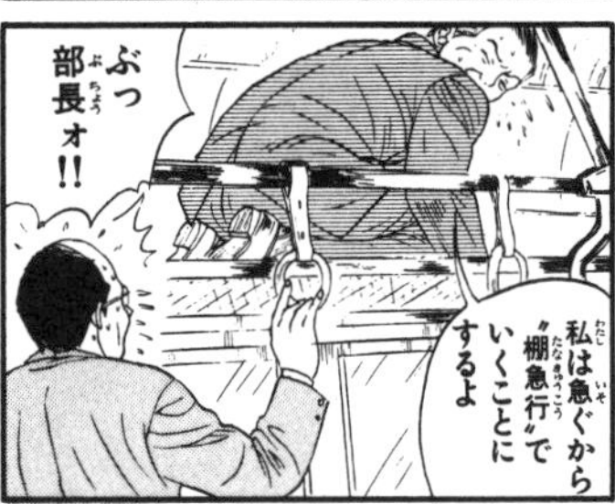

私は急ぐから"棚急行"でいくことにするよ
ぶっ部長ォ!!

Bucho: I'm in a hurry, so I'd better take the "Shelf Express."

Subordinate: B—Bucho!!

君はあとからゆっくり来たまえ
シュオオオ
部長ォ…

Bucho: You take your time and join me later.

FX: (shuooo) A sound of whooshing away.

Subordinate: Bucho...

…私としたことがちっとばかり甘かったかのォ…
ぶ…部長ォ!!

Bucho: I can't believe I didn't think of the consequences...

Subordinate: B—Bucho!!

Commentary:

• 部長 (bucho) is typically the title of an executive-class manager at a Japanese company. 甘い (amai) has various meanings, such as: 1) sweet; 2) not salted enough; 3) mild, indulgent or lenient; 4) easygoing or superficially optimistic; or 5) loose or not tight. When 部長 (bucho) used the word 甘い (amai) in panel #4, he meant that he could not believe that he had such unrealistic expectations.

• This is another example of how weird the author's sense of humor is.

柔道♡

JUDO♥

Girl: Ouch...

Girl: Oh no♥

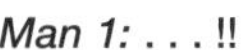

Man 1: . . . !!

い…生きててよかった!! こ…この感動オオオ!!
くそう…うらやましい…

Man 1: I—I'm glad I'm alive to witness this!! Wh—What a pleasure!!

Man 2: Shit... I envy him...

スケスケ先生 テニス編

SEE-THROUGH TEACHER, TENNIS EPISODE

FX: (ban) *A dramatic move.*

FX: (chira) *A quick and tiny flap.*

あぁ〜っパンツ見えたっ
もとからだってば

Fat Boy: Yay! I saw her panties.

Skinny Boy: But we always do.

バカァァーン!

FX: (bakaaan) *A loud smack.*

うひょ〜こんどは丸見えだ〜〜ッ
もとからだってばよ

Fat Boy: Whoaa, I saw the whole thing this time.

Skinny Boy: Like I said, we always do.

Commentary:

• いやあん (iyaan) is a feminine way of saying "oh no" or "no, don't." It can sound quite coquettish, and of course, Japanese men will find it sexy.

• For a middle-aged man, seeing a young girl half naked, with just a bra on, is exciting enough. いやあん (iyaan) certainly topped it off for him.

• Some readers will definitely think that the author has nailed the middle-aged Japanese man's fantasy in this comic strip.

Commentary:

• Yet again, the author is poking fun at the insatiable desire of boys who want to catch a glimpse of a girl's panties.

• The irony is that the fat boy is oblivious to the fact that See-Through Teacher's panties are always showing.

シリーズ

かわしまにっき

川島日記

Series

Kawashima's Diary

私の記憶が確かならば
キンキ30匹とカサゴ10匹とウニ10コ
尼さんは結構金づかいが荒い…

Right: If I remember correctly,

Nun: 30 kinki, 10 kasago, and 10 uni please.

Left: Nuns spend a good deal of money without any restraint...

Commentary:

• The official name for キンキ (kinki) is キチジ (kichiji). They're bright red fish, and along with 鯛 (tai), they are considered good luck food. カサゴ (笠子, kasago) look fierce, and due to their look, they used to be displayed at the Boys' Festival during the Edo Era. As mentioned earlier, ウニ (uni) is a spiny, hard-shelled animal whose fresh roe is considered a delicacy. キンキ (kinki), カサゴ (kasago) and ウニ (uni) are all pricey fish.

•Here are pictures of キンキ (kinki), カサゴ (kasago) and ウニ (uni):

宮史郎オンステージ

SHIRO MIYA ONSTAGE 1

Text: Shiro Miya On—OO Department—

Text: Women's Road.

Song: I've . . .

Song: given my love . . .

Song: to that man . . .

Commentary:

• 宮史郎 (Miya Shiro) is a well known singer, whose active career as a star reached its 40th anniversary in 1998. His unique, trademark hairstyle can easily be recognized by Japanese readers.

• "女のみち (onna no michi)" is one of his greatest hits. 女 (onna) means woman. みち (michi) means road or path.

Miya Shiro

由美かおる KAORU YUMI

FX: (zaba) *A loud splash.*

FX: (ho...) *A sigh.*

Woman: Something's wrong... No one's coming to peek...

Thoughts: I've seen enough of her...

Commentary:

• 由美かおる (yumi kaoru) is a Japanese actress whose career started in 1970s. She has appeared in numerous TV shows and movies over a couple of decades. Her roles included the sexy ninja type characters in period pieces. Now you know what makes this comic strip funny to many Japanese readers who have watched her over years.

断絶 SEVERANCE

Boy: I'm very serious about her!!

Boy: Please permit us to date!!

Man: No... I won't...

Boy: **Urrgh!!**

Text: My next door neighbor can't understand my true feelings...

FX: (poke) *Punch.*

Girl: It's too weird!! Don't do that!!

Commentary:

• Although it may appear quite old fashioned, in Japan it's still not unusual for a boy to meet a girl's parents and formerly ask for permission to date.

• The weird twist in this comic strip is the author's unique sense of humor.

銭湯の戦い

BATTLE IN THE BATHHOUSE

FX: (jiri jiri) *Slow, hesitant and timid movements.*

Woman: How long do you mean to stay there?

FX: (pen) *Slap.*

Woman: I can't clean up if you're there!!

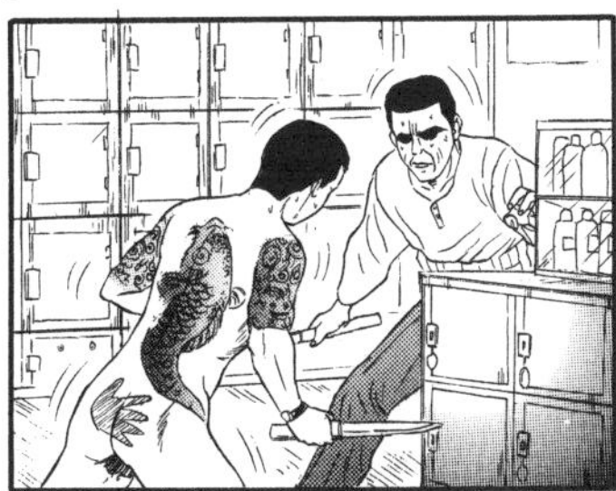

Woman: Didn't I tell you that you're in my way?

FX: (kan kan kan) *A series of sharp, high pitched sounds of whacking.*

Commentary:

• 銭湯 (sento) is the public bathhouse.

• From the tattoo, it's obvious that the two scary looking men are Yakuza. They are having a serious fight. Despite this fact, the woman who operates this 銭湯 (sento) doesn't seem to be frightened. Instead, she has no trouble attacking and getting rid of them—as if they're just a couple of annoying kids. It says a lot about how Yakuza and their antiquated style of fighting are viewed nowadays.

• Here is a picture of a typical 銭湯 (sento):

続おさなづま

CHILD BRIDE CONTINUES

Sachiko: C'mon, how can you play golf like that all the time?

Sachiko: You don't care about me at all!!

Sachiko: No more golf! No more!!

Recording: No more golf! No more!!

Husband: So she says...

Husband: My wife's really cute, you know.

Man: I—I don't envy you, okay!!

Commentary:

• This is another one of the おさな妻 (osanazuma) series.

• あたち (atachi) is a childish way of pronouncing the word あたし (atashi). あたし (atashi) is a feminine and more colloquial way of addressing someone. It comes from the more formal word わたし (watashi).

• The husband appears to adore Sachiko, but he doesn't act that way. The other men are envious of his young wife—who wouldn't be? Well, perhaps if the wife wasn't so young in reality, no one would—but in this series, the abnormality of the relationship is completely ignored. In other words, just laugh and accept it.

狂犬兄弟

MAD DOG BROTHERS

Aniki: I wonder what I should do in a situation like this...
Man: Leave this to me, Aniki!!

Man: Use the "everywhere door" that I built, and get away!!

Aniki: Er—Yeah!!

FX: (tosu) Opens easily.

Man: A—Aniki!! Argh!!
FX: (dogyu dogyu dogyu) *Ka-boom, ka-boom, ka-boom.*

Crowd: They're like mad dogs...

Commentary:

• どこでもドア (dokodemo doa) is one of the special tools used by an imaginary character called ドラえもん (doraemon). The ドラえもん (doraemon) series is the all-time hit children's manga classic in Japan. It was originally created in 1969-70 by Fujimoto Hiroshi and Motoo Abiko.

• When ドラえもん (doraemon) opens this どこでもドア (dokodemo doa) and says the name of the place he wishes to go, he will go there as he passes through it. The door itself looks like an old, nondescript wooden door.

• Also note, there is a movie called 狂犬三兄弟 (kyoken san kyodai), which translates to read "Three Mad Dog Brothers." It was first released in 1972. 菅原文太 (sugawara bunta) played the main role in this movie, and there is an uncanny likeness between Aniki and 菅原文太 (sugawara bunta). Apparently, the title of this comic strip originates from the movie.

スケスケ教師―ふれあい―

SEE-THROUGH TEACHER—COMMUNE

Teacher: Okay, it's done...

Teacher: Gya

FX: (makuri) *Pulling up.*

Student: Sensei, you're wearing white today!!

FX: (pun pun) *Getting upset.*

Teacher: What did you do that for, you ecchi!?

Teacher: Everyone's ecchi here at the boy's high school. What a problem it is!

Commentary:

• As mentioned earlier, エッチ(ecchi) is the Japanese pronunciation for the letter "H." This エッチ(ecchi) is derived from a Japanese word 破廉恥 (harenchi), which means infamy, shamelessness, ignominy or effrontery. When people say エッチ(ecchi), it usually has something to do with sex or lust.

• ぎゃっ (gya) is a short shriek of surprise.

• The student didn't need to pull up her skirt to see her panties because he could see it through her see-through skirt. In this comic strip, the author has captured the driving psychology behind the type of boys who can't help but pull up a girl's skirt. They do it simply to get the girls' attention.

シリーズ

かわしまにっき

川島日記

去年の春
ちょっと君……
ニタ
ニタ
ニタ
ニタ
ニタ
極左とまちがえられてつかまる……

Series

Kawashima's Diary

Right: Spring last year . . .

Police: Hey, you . . .

FX: (nita nita nita nita nita) *Grinning.*

Left: I was arrested because they mistook me for an extreme leftist . . .

Commentary:

• 去年 (kozo) can be read as "kyonen," and it means last year.

• You will find out exactly how this event has come about once you read the "End of Volume Bonus Part 2."

連作—春—新人教師

SERIES—SPRING—NEW TEACHER

Teacher: As of April, I will be teaching...

FX: (sawa sawa sawa) *A pleasant wind blowing.*

FX: (fuwaa...) *Lightly blow up.*

Teacher: Oh no♥

FX: (pachi pachi pachi pachi pachi pachi) *Clapping hands.*

Man 1: We haven't had a superstar like her for a while, have we?

Man 2: We'd better hold onto her.

Commentary:

• うかうか (ukauka) is a state of careless absentmindedness.

• These three middle-aged men reappear over and over. The author uses them as a tool to express the sensitivity of his generation with a sense of humor.

喧嘩仁義 ごろめんつう

RULES OF FIGHTING, GORO-MENTSU

Man 1: Are you ready...?

Man 2: Just a second...

Man 2: Please bear with me, Oyaji...

FX: (koto) *The light sound of an object being placed on the table.*

Man 2: I kept you waiting. Uryaaah

Man 1: O—Oh

Man 1: *That ball* bothers me...

Man 2: What the heck! You're totally help-less!!

Man 1: It'll fall... It'll fall..

FX: (doka doka doka) The loud sound of the kick.

連作—春—スケスケ先生

SERIES—SPRING SEE-THROUGH TEACHER

Teacher: Maybe it's because of the change of season. I caught a cold, you know.

FX: (sawa sawa) *A pleasant wind blowing.*

Boys: Teacher . . .

Teacher: It's cold!

FX: (sawa sawa) *A pleasant wind blowing.*

FX: (sawa sawa) *A pleasant wind blowing.*

FX: (sawa sawa) *A pleasant wind blowing.*

Text: The End

Commentary:

• There is a movie called 関東テキヤ一家喧嘩仁義ごろめんつう (kanto tekiya ikka kenkajingi goromentsu) released in 1970. The title of this comic strip is exactly the same as the latter half of the film's title. テキヤ (tekiya) is a racketeering type of Yakuza, and the film is about a fight between Yakuza families. The brothers in the movie are not blood relations, but rather, the brothers of the same crime family. 菅原文太 (sugawara bunta) played main role in this movie.

• ごろめんつう (goromentsuu) comes from ごろめんつ (goromentsu). ごろ (goro) is a Yakuza's lingo for 喧嘩 (kenka = fight). ごろめんつ (goromentsu) has pretty much the same meaning as 喧嘩仁義 (kenka jingi), which translates to read "rules of fighting."

• The author added another layer to this comic strip by including オヤジ (oyaji), the eyeball character from the classic anime ゲゲゲの鬼太郎 (gegege no kitaro). 目玉オヤジ (medama oyaji) is the father of the main character 鬼太郎 (kitaro), who fights and gets rid of evil monsters.

Commentary:

• The fact that she isn't wearing that infamous ブルマ (buruma) but instead, wearing some rolled up pants is enough to make the boys sink into despair. It's supposed to be a nice spring day with cherry flowers in full blossom...

• It's quite common to see cherry trees on school grounds. Here is a picture of a spring day with the cherry trees in full bloom, which is a common scene in Japan.

おさなづま3

CHILD BRIDE 3

Husband: I'm home, ha ha ha...

Husband: You've stayed up...

FX: (suu suu) *The steady, rhythmic sound of sleep—sound asleep.*

Husband: Ha ha ha, what kind'a food is this??

Husband: ...Did you cook it yourself...?

Text: Happy Birthday.

Husband: Why do I feel so guilty?

FX: (suu suu) *The steady, rhythmic sound of sleep—sound asleep.*

Commentary:

• This is another one of the おさな妻 (osanazuma) series.

• The husband comes home drunk—probably after he went out drinking with his co-workers. Perhaps, there are many men in Japan who either identify or sympathize with him.

連作—春—宮下先生

SERIES—SPRING MIYASHITA SENSEI

Song: I wonder where the bride will be taken away...

FX: (doki doki doki) *Throbbing heart*

Miyashita: I'm not that young anymore, so

Miyashita: don't look at me that closely please.

Man 1: She's unlike anyone we had before— a new type.

Man 2: Her careless approach is quite attractive . . .

Commentary:

• The song Miyashita's singing is a classic song called 花嫁人形 (hanayome ningyou) which was first released in 1923. 花嫁 (hanayome) means a bride, and 人形 (ningyou) means a doll. The lyrics of the song depict the children's perplexity over the brides who cry on the wedding day as they dress themselves for the wedding ceremony.

• In the old days before WWII, many young women had no choice over who they'd marry. Most of the marriages were arranged by the families, and even if a woman cared for someone else, she had to marry the person her family had chosen. If the woman and her lover could not bear being apart, it would often lead to a tragic outcome.

• The song is extremely sad, but fortunately, the brides nowadays aren't forced into this type of arranged marriage, so they tend not to feel the same way about their weddings.

連作—春—放課後

SERIES—SPRING AFTER-SCHOOL

FX: (sawa) *A pleasant wind blowing.*

Men: Ooh!

Girl: Oh no! ♥♥♥

FX: (buasa) *Quickly tuck under the curtain.*

Girl: Get out'a here, you guys! Right now!

Man 1: I have no regrets with my seishun!!!!

Man 2: N—No objections!!

Commentary:

• As mentioned earlier, 青春 (seishun) is a word used to describe the period of adolescence. "Don't have any regrets with your seishun" is a common phrase grownups use to warn young people not to waste this precious time in their lives that's full of vivid, heart-throbbing excitement.

• The boys look like high school students. This comic strip shows how naïve Japanese boys are (or used to be).

• With more and more images of explicit sex available through TV and movies, I can't imagine that boys in Western society would exhibit the same reaction that the boys in this comic strip do. In fact, this comic strip is probably showing how boys felt a generation ago. In other words, this comic strip is most likely derived from experiences the author had in his teens...

ももレンジャー3

PINK RANGER 3

Ranger: **Uryaah!!**

FX: (doka) *A hard kick.*

Ranger: **Toryaah!!**

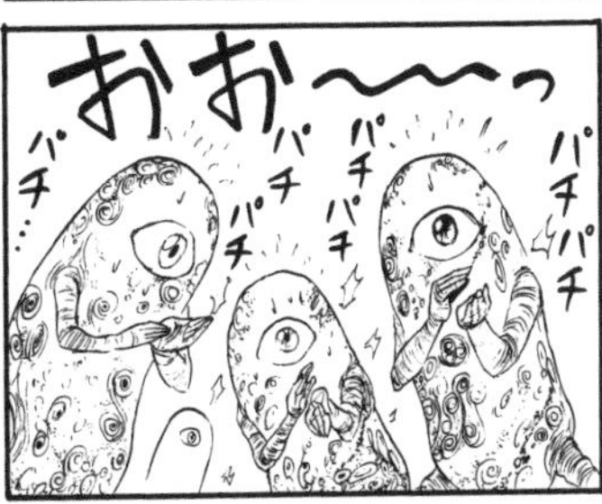

Monsters: **Ooooh**

FX: (pachi pachi pachi pachi...) *Clapping hands.*

Monster 1: That was the best costume so far, wasn't it!?

Monster 2: A pair of stockings and high heels—how excellent!!

Commentary:

•うりゃあ (uryaah) and とりゃあ (toryaah) are forceful Kiai-like yells of concentration.

• When you look at the word 心憎い (kokoro nikui), it sounds as if it might mean "hateful" since 心 (kokoro) means "heart" or "soul," while 憎い means "hate." However, 心憎い (kokoro nikui) has a completely different meaning from what you might expect. It means "tasteful, graceful or exquisite, as well as admirable, excellent or impressive."

熱海の夜

A NIGHT IN ATAMI

Man: I kept you waiting....?

FX: (suu suu) *The steady, rhythmic sound of sleep—sound asleep.*

FX: (suu suu) *The steady, rhythmic sound of sleep—sound asleep.*

Man: Already asleep, huh?

FX: (chira) *Peek.*

Man: Don't you wear the buruma!!

FX: (bibibin) A couple of loud slaps.

Woman: Oh no!!

Commentary:

• 熱海 (atami) with its traditional hot springs is one of the popular resorts in Japan. 熱 means hot and 海 means sea. The name 熱海 (atami) came about due to the ancient belief that the hot spring water originated from the sea. The city is surrounded by beautiful scenery, with Sagami Bay in the southeast and the Hakone mountains in the northwest. 熱海 (atami) has been a favorite destination for generations of Japanese and has attracted many honeymooners.

• It is obvious that the man has just come back from a nice dip in the hot spring. They are probably honeymooners. And, here again, the author's obsession over ブルマ (buruma) has been given another twist.

スケスケ番

SEE-THROUGH GANGS

Man: Ugh...

Woman: Thanks for giving us a hard time...

Woman: Let's go...

FX: (za za) *Heavy gait.*

Man: See-Through Gangs are frightening...

Commentary:

• スケスケ (suke suke) means see-through. スケ番 ban) is a word for a group of female delinquents. Obviously, the author played with the words スケスケ (suke suke) and スケ番 (suke ban) by combining them to read スケスケ番 (suke suke ban).

シリーズ
川島日記

朝起きたら
テレビで

三本足は
東

キュ
キュ

瀬川瑛子が
盲牌きっていた…

Series
Kawashima's Diary

Right: When I got up in the morning . . .

Woman: Three Legs are Ton (East)

FX: (kyu kyu) *A squeaky sound made by rubbing the tiles together.*

Left: Eiko Segawa was shuffling the blind tiles . . .

Commentary:

• 瀬川瑛子 (segawa eiko) is a Japanese singer.

• 盲牌 (moubai) is a term used in Mahjong, where a player can tell what tile it is just by the touch of it.

• The author is surprised to learn that she can do 盲牌 (moubai) without any problem.

ひぼたんばくと

HIBOTAN BAKUTO

FX: (do do do do do) *A loud sound reminiscent of a stampede.*

FX: (do do do do do) *A loud sound reminiscent of a stampede.*

Woman: I hereby take away your party boss' life.

Boss: **Ugyaaaah!!**

Text: Hibotan Bakuto

Text: The End

FX: (suta ta ta) *Quickly rushing away.*

Someone: P–Party boss!

Someone: Go! Go after her!!

Someone: Wait, you bitch!

Commentary:

• 緋 (hi) is deep and bright red. 牡丹 (botan) is a peony. 博徒 (bakuto) is a gambler-type Yakuza. There's a movie series called 緋牡丹博徒 (hibotan bakuto) made from 1968 to 1972. The movie 緋牡丹博徒 (hibotan bakuto) is also known as "Lady Yakuza," as well as "Red Peony Gambler." It's about the daughter of one of the Yakuza groups, whose father was killed by another group. The heroin of the movie wanders around Japan living the life of a gambler, until she fulfills her revenge.

• You may appreciate the author's touch in this parody—with the fully naked heroin.

中学生日記—昇華—

STUDENT'S DIARY—SUBLIMATION

うひょ〜〜〜 たまんねっ
丸見え だぜ〜
こ… こーなって たのか…

Boy 1: Uhyooh. Irresistible!

Boy 2: Totally visible there!

Boy 3: I—I didn't know it looked like that . . .

部活で発散だ〜〜ッ
うりゃ うりゃ
めっ めっ めっ

Boy 1: We'd better let off steam through the club activities.

Boy 2: Urya, urya!!

Boy 3: Men, men, men!!

うひゃ〜 たまんねぇ〜
モ… モロ見え じゃねえ かョ
あ〜なって たのかぁ〜

Boy 1: Uhyaah. Irresistible!

Boy 2: C—Completely visible there.

Boy 3: I didn't know that's what it looked like.

部活で発散だぁ〜ッ
うりゃ うりゃ
めっ めっ めっ

Boy 1: We'd better let off steam through the club activities.

Boy 2: Urya, urya!

Boy 3: Men, men, men!!

先生の秘密

DOCTOR'S SECRET

「今まで内緒にしていて すまん…実はな…」
「まあ なんですの 先生…」

Doctor: I'm sorry I kept this from you . . . As a matter of fact . . .

Nurse: Hmmm, what is it, Doctor?

「実は私は とべるのだよ」
「きゃあ 信じられないわ!!」

Doctor: In fact, I can fly.

Nurse: Kyaa. Unbelievable!!

「だから君のスカートも めくれちゃうってェ 寸法さ」
「まあ 先生 エッチね」
—完

Doctor: And, therefore, I can pull up your skirt too.

Nurse: Oh, Doctor, you're ecchi.

Text: The End

なんという さわやかな 読後感か!!
なんだか よくわかんねェけど オシャレだねっ

Boy 1: How refreshing it is to read something like this!

Boy 2: I don't know, but it's pretty hip.

Commentary:

• There is a TV show called 中学生日記 (chugakusei nikki), which translates to "Junior High School Students' Diary." The first episode was aired in 1972, and it's still on-air. Basically, it is a dramatized reality show (or, dramatized documentary film) with real students acting out scenes, depicting issues they have in their lives.

• うりゃ (urya) is a forceful Kiai-like yell of concentration. めっ (me) is short for 面 (men), which means face. By uttering 面 (men), a person is indicating that he is targeting the face of the opponent.

• I have a feeling that the boys' experience depicted in this comic strip won't ever make it into the TV version of the 中学生日記 (chugakusei nikki).

Commentary:

• Here's another one of theビニ本 (bini hon) series. As I mentioned earlier, ビニ本 (bini hon) is the plastic covered magazine sold through vending machines in the 1970s. This genre of magazine is currently called エロ本 (erohon), which is a type of magazine that generally appeals to the carnal desires of the male population. They are now sold without plastic covers.

• 先生 (sensei) is a commonly used term for addressing someone with respect. Usually, it's used to address people like teachers, professors, lawyers, doctors and politicians.

はんば　はな
飯場の花3

FLOWER OF THE CONSTRUCTION CAMP 3

おまたせェ みなさん お茶ですょ
おう

Girl: Sorry about making you wait. It's time for a tea break, everyone.

Man: Yeah.

Girl: Humph, they were heavy.

今 私の胸を 感動のさざなみが襲う…
お… 親方!!

Boss: A wave of excitement is welling up inside me right now . . .

Man: B—Boss!!

我が人生 一片の 悔いなし!!
がしっ
同感です 親方ァ!!

Boss: I have no regrets in my life!!

FX: (gashi) *Hold tight.*

Man: I feel the same, Boss!!

Commentary:

• 花 (hana) means flower, but it can refer to a beautiful female that attracts attention. 飯場 (hanba) is a place where mine or construction workers temporarily live together on the site. Just as I previously mentioned, it's similar to the phrase 紅一点 (kouitten), 飯場の花 (hanbano hana), which refers to a single woman among rough guys. Nowadays, 飯場の花 (hanbano hana) is sometimes used to mean a woman who cooks meals.

• I would like to mention the Japanese slang, パンチラ (panchira). パン (pan) is short for panties and チラ (chira) comes from ちらり (chirari), which means "to catch a glimpse of." In this comic strip, the author is playing upon the Japanese men's fetish for パンチラ (panchira).

毛抜きの哲学

PHILOSOPHY OF PULLING HAIR

Girl 1: When you look at the hair on the leg carefully,
Girl 1: you'll notice ones that are red around their roots like this one.

Text: Expanded image.

Girl 1: Surprisingly, it doesn't hurt at all to pull them out!!
Girl 1: In fact, they give a pleasant sensation.
FX: (kui kui) *Pulling by force.*

Girl 2: Wow, that's incredible.
Girl 1: Ho ho ho...
Girl 1: It's the result of my long-standing research, you know.

Boy: I've overheard my sister's incredible secret...

Boy: What should I do?

Commentary:

• It used to be uncommon in Japan for any woman to shave her legs. It's only about a decade or two since women have begun to shave their legs—and I'm sure, many Japanese girls still don't shave them. So, it's not all that strange for some Japanese girls to obsess over the hair on their legs.

• What's funny is the naiveté of the boy, who thinks that what he overheard was so embarrassingly sacred that he is at a loss as to what to do.

カムイとズンムたち

KAMUI AND ZUNMU

Kamui: Oh no! ♥

Zunmu 1: What do you mean by "oh no," Kamui...?

FX: (wana wana) *Quivering with anticipation or excitement.*

Zunmu 2: You mean, you've deceived us up until now?

Zunmu 1: You mean, you are a woman, Kamui?

Everyone: Ooh!

Zunmu: (gue he he he he) Sleazy snigger.
FX: (do do do do do) *A loud sound reminiscent of a stampede.*
Kamui: No!
Text: I've heard that the assassins found new meaning in their lives.
Text: All's well that ends well.

Commentary:

• There is a manga by 白土三平 (shirato sanpei) called カムイ外伝 (kamui gaiden). It is a series that was first published in 1965. The series was made into anime and first aired in 1969. The title eventually changed to カムイ伝 (kamui den), which translates to "The Legend of Kamui." This manga/anime has become a classic, and new prints are still released along with new episodes.

• In that manga/anime series, Kamui is a boy who escapes from a Ninja organization, which is a forbidden act. Thus, the organization sends a series of assassins after him.

茂吉の願い

MOKICHI'S WISH

おとなりのおじいちゃん
おやまあ…

Girl: My neighbor, Ojii-chan.

Mokichi: Oh, boy...

Girl: Here's a circulating notice.

Mokichi: Young lady, who are you?

Girl: I am a bear!!

Girl: Gaoh!!

Mokichi: Hyaa, I'm scared.

Mokichi: Ha ha ha

Man: How was my wife?

Mokichi: I have no regrets. Thank you...

Commentary:

• おじいちゃん(ojii-chan) is equivalent to the English word "Grandpa," but it can be used to address any old man, whether the old man is your relative or a complete stranger.

• がおーっ (gaoh) sounds like an animal growl. ひゃあ (hyaa) is a short shriek of fright.

• 思い残すことはない (omoi nokosu koto ha nai) is a phrase that is used to indicate that the person is so satisfied that he/she has nothing to regret, even if he/she died right there and then.

重心

CENTER OF GRAVITY

Boy: Center of gravity.

Girl: Stop! Stop it!

Boy: Center of gravity.

FX: (yoro yoro) *Wavering.*

Girl: Stop! Stop it!

Boy: Center of gravity.

FX: (yoro yoro) *Wavering.*

Girl: Stop! Stop it!

FX: (don) *Bang!!*

FX: (gashaan) *A loud crash.*

Commentary:

• 重心 (jushin) means center of gravity. If you split the word in two and swap the position of the characters, it can read "shinju," although there is no such word as 心重 (shinju). However, there is a word 心中 (shinju) which means a double suicide, where lovers or family members commit suicide together.

• In this comic strip, it appears that the author played with the words 重心 (jushin) and 心中 (shinju) by having the lovers play with gravity that ends up killing them both.

廊下に立ってなさい松崎君

STAND OUTSIDE THE CLASS, MATSUZAKI-KUN

Sensei: ...Matsuzaki, go stand outside the class!!

Matsuzaki: No, I won't!!

Song: Cha la la la laaa, cha la la la laaa la

FX: (chira chira) *Flick discreetly.*

Matsuzaki: Ooh!!

FX: (gata) *A dull thud, indicating that the chair made a noise when he stood up.*

FX: (su su su) *Swiftly move away.*

FX: (su su su) *Swiftly move away.*

Matsuzaki: Ooh!!

Song: Cha la la la la laaa la laaa la laaa

Matsuzaki: Sensei, you used that dirty trick again!

Sensei: Ho ho ho, you're so easy to trick, Matsuzaki.

Commentary:

• The Kanji character 色 (iro) has many different meanings that include: 1) color; 2) complexion, countenance; 3) love, romance; 4) carnal desire, lust, sensual pleasure; 5) a person's sex appeal; 6) variety. 仕掛け (shikake), in this instance, means trick or gimmick. So, the word 色仕掛け (irojikake) means a trick that takes advantage of men's carnal desires.

• Here, the author is poking fun at boys' sexual curiosity.

シリーズ
ひとコマ番外地

ゴッコ
（資料なし）

骨がないお魚
鍋物にしたら
美味しい
らしいけど
身もほとんどない

Series
Irregular One Panel Page

Gokko
(No reference materials)

Fish without bones.

It's supposed to be tasty to eat in a hot pot, but it hardly has any meat to eat.

Commentary:

• This information about Gokko will be useful when you read the comic strip entitled GLUTTONS BANZAI!!

ゴッコ (gokko)

イェーイ イェーイ

YEAH, YEAH

Song: Crown, crown girls...

Song: Loads of them, loads of them...

FX: (moji moji) *Nervous and hesitant move.*

Song: Yeah, yeah, yeaah...

FX: (moji moji) *Nervous and hesitant move.*

Man: Be more serious!

FX: (paan) The high-pitched sound of a slap.

Boy: B—But...!!

食いしん坊万才!!

GLUTTONS BANZAI!!

Man: I hear Gokko is a fish without any bones.

Old Woman: So I hear.

Man: What is the secret for cooking it?

Old Woman: Nothing.

Man: ...

Man: See you next week.

Music: Cha cha la chaaa, poke poke

Text: The End

Commentary:

• This is a parody of a TV commercial for underwear and sanitary napkins. The original song was written by 小林亜星 (kobayashi asei), and its light touch made it perfectly fine to be aired on any TV channel at any time of the day.

• It was part of a TV commercial campaign called ワンサカ娘 (wansaka musume) for Renown, an apparel maker. It was so successful that the ワンサカ娘 (wansaka musume) commercial campaign was aired from 1961 through the early 1980s. The ワンサカ娘 (wansaka musume) campaign's undisputable success is also evidenced by the fact it is now available as a music CD.

• It's just that the commercial is made for the female consumer. It won't work as commercial for guy's underwear and condoms—urrgh—and definitely not on any channel at any time of the day.

Commentary:

• 食いしん坊万才 (kuishinbo banzai) is a Japanese TV show where a glutton visits restaurants, inns, chefs, and individuals to taste something special and discuss the food. Usually, he has a lot to say about the food he tastes.

• The word 美味しい (oishii), which means "delicious," is often heard during the show. However, in this comic strip, the author pokes fun at the show by creating a situation where the glutton has a hard time making conversation on-air—and he can't even utter the trademark exclamation 美味しい (oishii).

こっちおいでよ

COME TO ME

Mother: Come to me, Sacchan.

Sacchan: (yah yah) *No, no!!*

Mother: Ah, he's scary, isn't he? But it's okay now.

Sacchan: Kya, kya!!

Father: You know...

Sacchan: Kya, kya, kya!!

Father: I think my daughter-in-law dislikes me...

Text: The End

Commentary:

• This is the extension of the おさな妻 (osanazuma = Child Bride) series. Please note that there is no mention of the word おさな妻 (osanazuma) here. You'll later notice that the concept develops into something beyond the initial idea sparked by the concept of おさな妻 (osanazuma) and becomes the so called Sacchan series.

• キャッ キャッ (kya kya) is a series of short giggles.

• 嫁 (yome) means bride, but it is often used to refer to a daughter-in-law who lives with the husband's parents.

ちゅうがくせいにっき 中学生日記2

STUDENT'S DIARY

Text: Missed.

Boy 1: I wonder how many times I have to try before I get the right one.

Boy 2: It looks like you got the right one this time...

Boy 1: What!? Show me! Show me!!

Text: Right on.

Boy 2: Why don't you give up!? Okay?

Commentary:

• As I mentioned earlier, there is a TV show called 中学生日記 (chugakusei nikki), which translates to read "Junior High School Students' Diary." It is a dramatized reality show (or dramatized documentary film) with real students acting out the scenes that depict issues they have in their lives.

• I'm sure boys in Japan share similar experiences to the one shown here, but you can be certain this will never make it into the TV version of the 中学生日記 (chugakusei nikki), and that's what makes it so funny.

ジェットコースター

JET COASTER

FX: (go go go go go) *A grumbling sound.*

Crowd: Kyah, kyah!!

Crowd: Kyah, kyah!!

FX: (goh) *A rumble reminiscent of a jet airplane powering up.*

FX: (doon) An explosive bang.

Someone: Whoaah!! Mitsukuni!!

Someone: Kyaaah!! Arisa-chan!!

FX: (waaa waaa waaa) *The agitated noise of the crowd.*

Commentary:

• キャー キャー (kyah, kyah) is a scream of excitement and delight.

• 光国 (mitsukuni) is a boy's name and 悪里沙 (arisa) is a girl's name.

• Read the title and you'll get the point.

酒呑みの知恵

DRINKER'S WISDOM

Man 1: Oh... it's drinker's wisdom, isn't it?

Man 2: Human flesh, human flesh...

Man 1: I'd love to partake of some of it later...

Man 2: Before it gets cold. Before it gets cold...

FX: (hoka hoka) *Nice and warm.*

Man 2: Yoshiko, please come back...

Commentary:

• It's common to warm up sake before drinking. The wisdom of this sake drinker is to warm up the big bottle of sake in what appears to be a traditional hot spring. Warming up sake so that it is roughly the same temperature as the human body is a good idea—but the true wisdom that this man espouses, which the second man does not see, is that the warm bottle of sake is used as a replacement for 美子 (Yoshiko). In other words, the sake is comforting him like 美子 (Yoshiko) would have done. And, of course, 美子 (Yoshiko) is probably the man's wife or lover who left him.

ひぼたんばくと2

HIBOTAN BAKUTO 2

Woman: Please use this one...

Man 1: Thank you for your kindness...

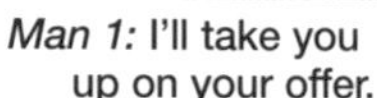

Man 1: I'll take you up on your offer.

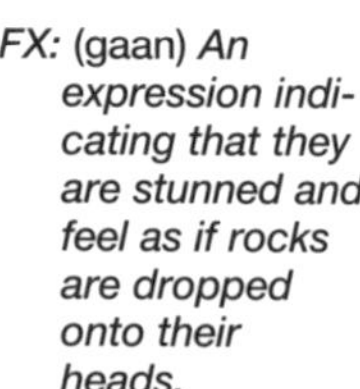

FX: (gaan) *An expression indicating that they are stunned and feel as if rocks are dropped onto their heads.*

Text: Hibotan Bakuto—To Be Continued.

Man 2: We won't forgive you! Not after that!

FX: (dosu dosu) *A series of loud, heavy blows.*

Man 1: Ugyaaaaaah

Commentary:

• 使っておくんなまし (tsukatte okun namashi) is 使って下さい (tsukatte kudasai), and ごっつうすんまへん (gottsuu sunmahen) is 大変すみません (taihen sumimasen) in 関西弁 (kansaiben = the Kansai dialect). うぎゃああああ (ugyaaaaaah) is a shriek of pain.

• As I mentioned earlier, there's a series of movies called 緋牡丹博徒 (hibotan bakuto) that were made from 1968 to 1972. The movie 緋牡丹博徒 (hibotan bakuto) is also known as "Lady Yakuza," as well as "Red Peony Gambler." It is clearly another parody of 緋牡丹博徒 (hibotan bakuto) done in the author's unique style.

贈る言葉

GIFT OF WORDS

FX: (kacho kacho kacho...) *Click, click, click...*

Homeless: Ooh... here it is...

Text: It's a nice sunny day at Gotanda — from Masa

Homeless: I see... He too has left Shinjuku after all.

Homeless: Good luck...

Commentary:

• 贈る言葉 (okuru kotoba) is the title of a famous song. It is a song about the tender words a man says at the time of parting from his first and unrequited love. The theme of this song is especially appealing to youth who are about to graduate from school (when all students part their ways), and it is often sung by many at the time of graduation—especially at informal parties.

• When you visit Tokyo, you'll witness many homeless people in the 新宿 (Shinjuku) area. If you read between the lines, you'll realize that Masa is also a homeless man, who has left the 新宿 (Shinjuku) area and moved to another part of Tokyo called 五反田 (gotanda).

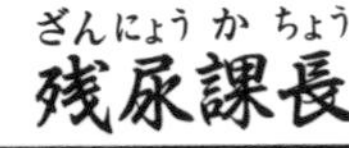

LEFTOVER PEE SECTION CHIEF

Text: There was an old section chief nicknamed "Leftover Pee Section Chief."

Chief: Hm?

Chief: Oooh oh ooooh

Chief: Oooh oooh oooooh!!

Text: No one has seen him since...

Text: — The End

Commentary:

• Although it might not be the norm any longer, traditional Japanese companies used to boast of lifelong employment. With that as the backdrop, the author is poking fun at this situation—where an aging white-collar manager is given an unpalatable name after he hangs onto his job until he can no longer function properly.

シリーズ
かわしまにっき
川島日記
お客とのコミュニケーションも大切だ
貝はうけ口だから大きい方が下です
へぇ〜っ

Series Kawashima's Diary

Right: It's important to communicate with the customers.

Man: Shellfish have protruding lower lips, and therefore the bigger side should be the bottom.

Customer: (heh) Hmmm

Commentary:

• へぇーっ (heh) is a type of exclamation indicating that a person is impressed by understanding or perceiving something new.

• Here the author makes fun of how he and his customers all stick out their lower lips, as he explains the anatomy of the shellfish.

ドラマ おさな母(はは)

DRAMA, CHILD MOTHER

Mother: I beg you, please not this money!!

Son: Shut up. You give that to me, old hag!!

Son: Urya!!

FX: (tei) *There!!*

FX: (koron) *Roll over.*

Mother: Kya

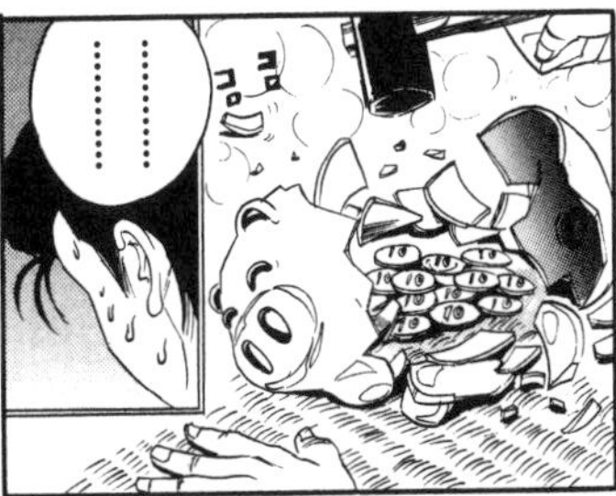

FX: (koro koro) *Roll out.*

Mother: (shiku shiku shiku) Suppressed sob.

Son: What am I doing...?

Commentary:

• This is another variation to the おさな妻 (osanazuma = Child Bride) series. It is more or less a precursor to the Sacchan series that's introduced later on.

放課後の恋人たち

AFTER-SCHOOL LOVERS

Girl: There!

FX: (koki koki) The sound of popping bones.

Girl: Ouch...

Girl: Somehow, I managed...

Girl: How's this, Bucho?

FX: (chira) *A quick glance.*

Girl: Kyaa!!

Girl: That's what you meant to do from the get go?

Girl: Geez, Bucho, how ecchi you are!!

Commentary:

• 部長 (bucho), in this instance, is the title given to someone who heads an after-school club or extra curricular activity called 部活 (bukatsu).

• In this comic strip, it looks like they're members of an art club.

• This is another example of the author poking fun at the insatiable desire of boys to catch a glimpse of girls' panties.

茂吉の涙

MOKICHI'S TEARS

Girl: Let me sing.

Song: I miss Anju, ho yare ho...

Song: I miss Zushio, ho yare ho...

Girl: Ojii-chan, please recover from your cold soon, and . . .

Girl: be healthy again. The end.

FX: (pekori) *Bow.*

Yosaburo: How was my wife?

Mokichi: I have no regrets. Thank you, Yosaburo...

Commentary:

• あんじゅ (anju, 安寿) and ずしおう (zushio, 厨子王) are characters in the legendary oral tradition which was eventually made into a novel by 森鴎外 (mori ougai) in 1915.

• There's also a movie called 山椒大夫 (sansho dayu), whose English title is "Sansho the Bailiff." The film was made in 1954. The tragic story is set in 11th century Japan, where 安寿 (anju) and 厨子王 (zushio) are separated from their mother after being ambushed by the evil antagonist. Their mother is sold as a prostitute, while 安寿 (anju) and 厨子王 (zushio) are sold as slaves. The song the girl is singing appears to express the sad feelings the mother has after being separated from her children.

• ほーやれほ (ho yare ho) is a rhythmic shout to keep the song going.

ひぼたんばくと3

HIBOTAN BAKUTO 3

FX: (shaka shaka) *The rattling sound of the bicycle.*

Woman: Will you please wait!!

Woman: You're going away no matter what?

Man: Yup....

Woman: I suppose there's no use in trying to stop you then.

Woman: Please don't forget me...

FX: (jiii) Staring hard.

名前を呼んで

CALL MY NAME

Woman: What do you want...?

Sachiko: E he he, I brought you some snacks.

Woman: You're a bit too much.

Woman: Please don't enter my room as if it's yours!!

FX: (pishan) *The sharp, high-pitched sound of a door shutting.*

Husband: Sachiko.

Sachiko: She wouldn't call me Oneh-san.

Sachiko: (waa) Crying out loud.

Husband: I'm sorry you have to suffer so much.

Commentary:

• This is another parody of 緋牡丹博徒 (hibotan bakuto) done with the author's unique sense of humor.

• Please note that the movie 緋牡丹博徒 (hibotan bakuto) is set in an era before bicycles were introduced in Japan.

• Also look at panel #4 -- did you notice the pieces of curly hair sticking onto the seat of the bicycle? Keep in mind the author's sense of humor and just imagine what this means...

Commentary:

• This is one of the おさな妻 (osanazuma = Child Bride) series. It is more or less a precursor to the Sacchan series called けものみち (kemonomichi), which translates to read "Animal Trail," that's introduced later on.

楢山節考 THE BALLAD OF NARAYAMA

Tatsuhei: Mother!!

Tatsuhei: Mother, it's snowing. How lucky you are!

FX: (do do do do do) *A grumbling sound.*

Mother: I'll see you again on the next planet, Tatsuhei...

Father: Where did you leave your mother? You, undutiful son!!

Tatsuhei: P—Please ask nothing...

Commentary:

• 楢山節考 (narayama bushiko) is a film made in 1980s and is known as "The Ballad of Narayama." The story is set in the late 1800s, in a poor mountain village where families exist on a subsistence level and accept the cruelties of life. In the story, 辰平 (tatsuhei)'s old mother chooses to go to 楢山 (narayama) to die. 辰平 (tatsuhei) respects his mother's wish and helps her carry out her plan. Snow falls as his mother sits at 楢山 (narayama) to die, while 辰平 (tatsuhei) returns home. 辰平 (tatsuhei) is sad but also pleased that his mother achieved her goal while his father regards it with horror.

• The author successfully encapsulated the final scene of the move in this comic strip.

チーママ CHEE-MAMA

Man: Oh no, I spilled, and I'm soaking wet...

Woman: Chee-Mama!

Chee-Mama: Oh dear, it's not good. Ho ho ho ho

Chee-Mama: It'll stain your pants. Why don't you take them off!!

FX: (puri puri) *Sexy hip swing.*

Man: N—No, it's okay. It's nothing.

Chee-Mama: It'll stain your pants. Why don't you take them off!!

FX: (puri puri) Sexy hip swing

Man: ...I mean it. It's okay. Okay?

Commentary:

• Usually a female manager of a bar in Japan is called ママ (mama) and another female who's next in command is called チ_ママ (chii mama).

• How can the man take off his pants? The sexy チ_ママ (chii mama) in her see-through kimono is right in front of him with her hips swinging in such a provocative way. Look at where his hands are, and you can imagine the state he's in.

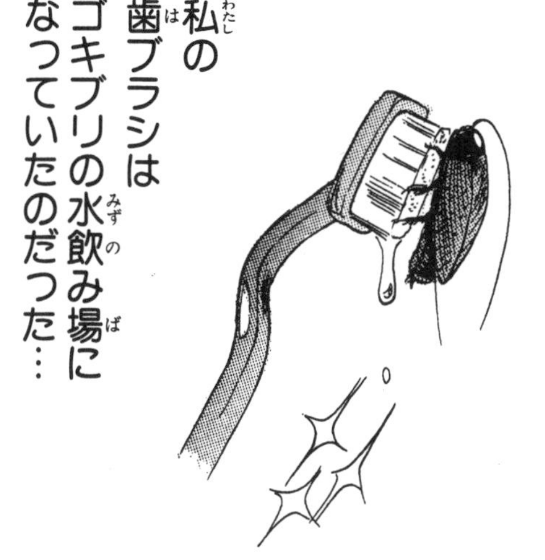

シリーズ
川島日記
朝の詩
すっかり
忘れていた…
私の
歯ブラシは
ゴキブリの水飲み場に
なっていたのだった…

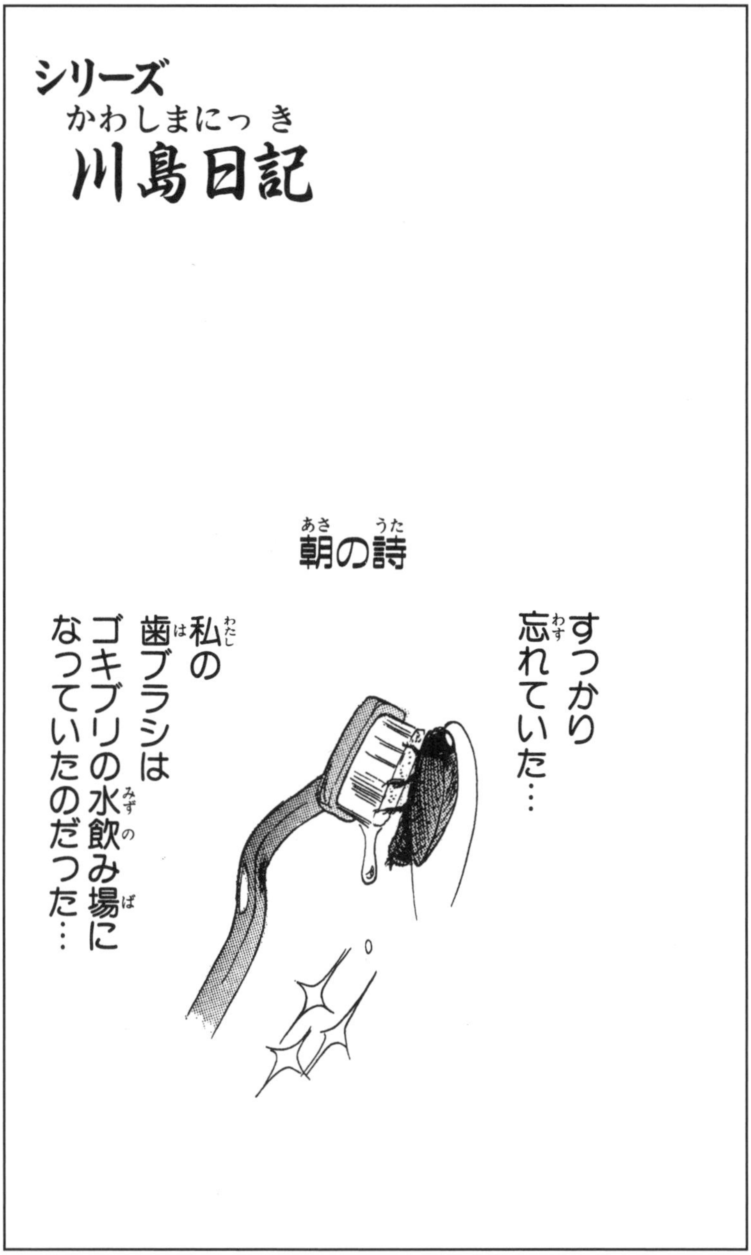

Series
Kawashima's Diary

Morning Ballad

Right: I totally forgot...

Left: My toothbrush has become the cockroach's watering place...

Commentary:

• Yuck! Laugh and say no more....

夢 (ゆめ)

DREAM

その夜は
空を飛ぶ夢をみた

Text: That night,

Text: I dreamed of flying through the sky.

Someone: Carry him without getting his vomit on us!!

Someone: Geez, what a nuisance he is...!

Text: A cool breeze was blowing, and

Text: it was a pleasant dream.

Someone: Ah, I can't do it.

Someone: Let's leave him alone for a while...

Commentary:

• ゲロ (gero), in this instance, is slang for vomit.

• Obviously the guy has passed out while barfing. The disparity between the dream and the reality—sounds familiar, right?

宮下先生の生活 (みやしたせんせい せいかつ)

MIYASHITA SENSEI'S LIFE

Husband: C'mon, let's play dolls. C'mon!

Wife: Ka-boom, ka-boom.

Wife: Whoosh, du-bang.

Husband: Ooh!!

Wife: They both died.

Wife: The end.

Husband: Urrrgh!!

FX: (gakkushi) Fall down weakly, disappointed.

Wife: Why did I marry a kid like him...?

FX: (kachi...) *Click...*

Commentary:

• The humor is the same as the おさな妻 (osanazuma) series—it's just that, instead of a juvenile wife, she's got a juvenile husband.

おそうじ

CLEANING

FX: (goshi goshi) *Scrub, scrub.*

FX: (jororo joro . . .) *The sound of spurting urine.*
FX: (puri puri) *Sexy hip swing.*

FX: (puri puri) *Sexy hip swing.*
FX:(choro choro choro) *The sound of leaking.*

FX:(puri puri) *Sexy hip swing.*

FX:(choro choro choro choro choro . . .) *The sound of dripping.*

Commentary:

• The boy has to urinate pretty badly, but the trouble is, there's this girl showing her panties. And when she swings her hips in such a provocative way, it makes it nearly impossible. How can he relax and urinate with this going on?

のぞいちゃだめよ

IT'S NOT OKAY TO PEEK

Woman: Ah!

Woman: It's not okay to peek, little boy.

Husband: E he he.

Husband: The next door neighbor's wife has a nice body.

Husband: Gu he he . . .

Wife: What're you grinning at as you eat . . .?

Commentary:

• えへへ (e he he) is an innocent chuckle, while ぐへへ (gu he he) is a sleazy chortle.

• The Gloom Party falls under the genre of "nonsense gags," in which readers are often left wondering what it (the comic strip) means. In the "nonsense gag," there might and might not be any hidden point. Readers can even create their own meaning, which may have nothing to do with what was in the author's mind when the comic strip was created.

• The way the little boy (husband) speaks on panel #4 sounds as if a grown man has said the words. It is hardly a child talk. Thus, the readers could be left wondering if there was a deeper meaning to this comic strip. This is a classic representation of the "nonsense gag."

てんこうせい
転校生!!

TRANSFERRED STUDENT

FX: (pachi pachin pachin) *Snapping fingers.*

FX: (pachi pachi pachi pachin) *Snapping fingers.*

FX: (pachin pachin pachin pachin) *Snapping fingers.*

Girl: They're notorious bad guys!! It's better you don't get involved with them!!

Boy: Ku u u!!

Commentary:

• くうう (ku u u) is a growling sort of sound, and in this instance, it indicates the boy's frustration.

• This is a parody of the "West Side Story." Need I say more?

ていしゅ
ガキ亭主

KID HUSBAND

Husband: (een een) *Crying.*

Husband: (een een) *Crying.*

Wife: I dreamed of him crying..

Wife: It's bad. I wonder if something's happened to him . . .

Wife: Oh no, I was using him as my pillow!!

FX: (gaan) An expression indicating that she is stunned and feels as if a rock has been dropped on her head.

Husband: (uun uun) *Groaning.*

Commentary:

• It is human nature to think that one's dream carries some sort of message, isn't it?

へんしんかんりょう
変身完了

TRANSFORMATION'S COMPLETE

FX: (shuu) *A steamy sort of sound.*

FX: (shuu) *A steamy sort of sound.*

Ranger: Alright! Transformation's complete.

FX: (pachi pachi pachi pachi . . .) *Clapping hands.*

Monster 1: It's great to watch—no matter how often I see her do it.

Monster 2: She intentionally slowed down. What a touching performance.

Commentary:

• This is another ももレンジャー (momo renjaa) series, which reminds us of the well-known TV show "Power Rangers."

• In this particular comic strip, the author combined other TV anime series, something like "Sailor Moon," in which a female protagonist routinely goes through a transformation process in each episode. The transformation involves magically stripping off her clothes and putting on a special garment.

3秒 — THREE SECONDS

やーーん 信じらん なーーい
んじゃ もう1回 やっか!?
え〜〜

Girl: No way, I can't believe it.

Boy 1: Let's try once more then, huh!?

Boy 2: What!?

FX: (pu) *Pull out.*

おっ!?
な!?
こいつ あごひげ 抜くと3秒間 気絶すんだ

Boy 2: Oh!?

Boy 1: See!?

Boy 1: He faints for three seconds after a hair is pulled from his chin.

やーーん 信じらん なぁい
んじゃ もう1回 やっか!?
え〜〜

Girl: No way, I can't believe it.
Boy 1: Let's try once more then, huh!?
Boy 2: What!?

Commentary:

• It is obvious that the scene is taking place at a school. Girls are wearing the school uniform. The boys are also wearing the school uniform, except the chubby one has taken off his school jacket. You can glimpse a black school bag hanging by the side of the desk.

• As to the content of this comic strip—enjoy the weirdness of it for all it's worth.

じっくり拝みな — TAKE A GOOD LOOK

やいやい!! この彫モンが 見えねェの かよう!!

Girl: Hey, hey!! Can you see my tattoo, huh!?

背中だョ 背中ァ!!

Girl: It's on my back. On my back!!

ほらョ じっくりと 拝みなっ

Girl: Here, take a good look.

こっちじゃ ねえって 言ってる だろォ

Girl: I told you, it's not on this side.

Commentary:

• The way the girl speaks is more like the way a male Yakuza would talk. じっくり拝みな (jikkuri ogamina), which means "take a good look," is the type of phrase a Yakuza might use when telling someone to look at his tattoo, in an attempt to both impress and shock the person.

• In this comic strip, the author shows how even the notorious Yakuza men cannot escape their sexuality. Please note the bumps on the men's heads in panel #3 and #4, as well as the bloody nose spurting from one of the men. Clearly the girl has beaten them up, but still, the men can't help themselves.

むごんげき
無言劇

PANTOMIME

Boy/Girl: Kid!!

Commentary:

• ガキ (餓鬼, gaki) is a derogatory word that means “kid” with scornful overtones. The Kanji character 餓 (ga) means hunger, and 鬼 (oni) is an imaginary creature similar to a demon, ogre or goblin. The word 餓鬼 (gaki) is originally used in Buddhism, where it refers to the dead who must suffer hunger and thirst due to evil deeds committed while alive.

• Please note that it’s the kids themselves who call the other kid ガキ (gaki), instead of the grown spouses.

ざんにょう
残尿さん

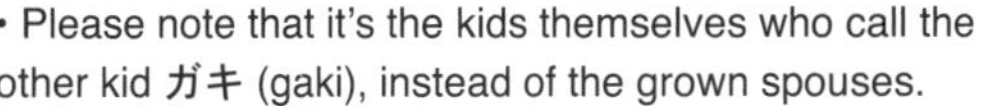

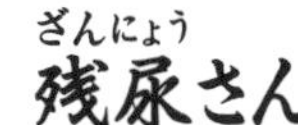

MR. LEFTOVER PEE

Woman 1: Oh, there goes Mr. Leftover Pee.

Woman 2: Oh dear.

Man: Hm?

Man: Oooh oh ooooh

Man: Oooh oooh oooooh!!

Woman 1: Right at 3:50 PM again today . . .

Woman 2: Oh dear . . .

Commentary:

• In this “Leftover Pee” series, the author continues to poke fun at an aging man. Just as the idea of urinating fascinates young children, who might have just gotten out of diapers, it continues to fascinate different generations.

シリーズ

川島日記

口でとけずに
手の脂でとける
ナマコの神秘
いつか解明したい

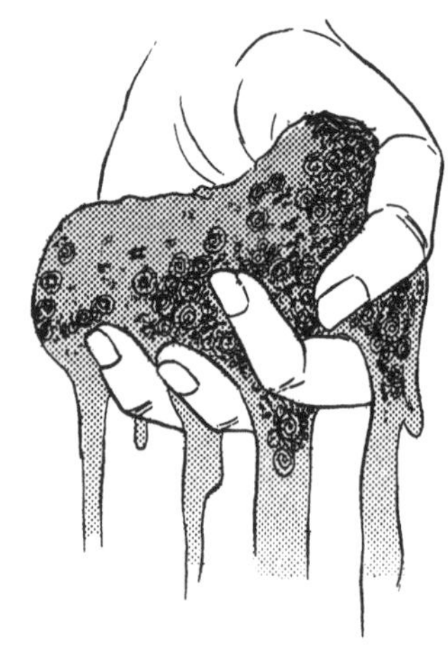

Series

Kawashima's Diary

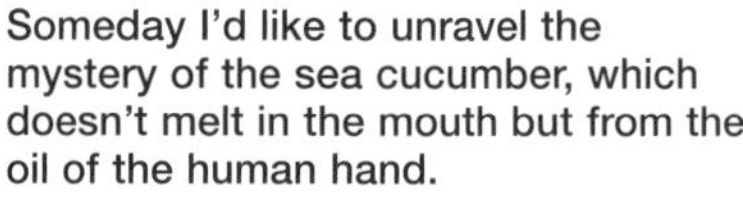

Someday I'd like to unravel the mystery of the sea cucumber, which doesn't melt in the mouth but from the oil of the human hand.

Commentary:

• ナマコ (namako = sea cucumbers) are cylinder-shaped invertebrates, with elongated, leathery, muscular bodies. They have no appendages and remind people of a rotten cucumber.

• Fishermen or fishmongers (like the author used to be) are the type of people who tend to dwell on this type of odd mystery.

•Here is a picture of a ナマコ (namako):

カムイとズンムたち2

KAMUI AND ZUNMU 2

Text: Summary.

Text: Once Kamui was revealed to be a woman, she was pursued relentlessly.

FX: (sara sara) *The sound of a peacefully flowing river.*

FX: (sara sara sara) *The sound of peacefully flowing river.*

Zunmu 1: That Kamui . . . She's wearing white today!!

FX: (doki doki) *Throbbing heartbeat.*

Zunmu 2: She was wearing polka dots yesterday.

Zunmu 3: I told you to capture her!!

FX: (dokaa) *A heavy blow.*

その後の残尿課長1

LEFTOVER PEE SECTION CHIEF AFTERWARDS 1

Text: Leftover Pee Section Chief has reached his retirement.

Chief: Hm?

Chief: Ooh oh ooh

Chief: Ooh oh ooooh

Woman: Do it in the bathroom!!

FX: (poke) Punch.

Text: He didn't get along well with his daughter-in-law.

Commentary:

• ズンム (zunmu) is an old, discriminatory word (which most Japanese are not familiar with). It means sons who are not the first son. やっこ (yakko) is another word which is equivalent to ズンム (zunmu). These words were used in the rural parts of the 東北 (tohoku) region, during the time Samurai were still around. It was quite common at that time for poor farmers to favor their first sons. The rest of their sons, the ズンム (zunmu), were forsaken. ズンム (zunmu) wore tattered clothes, let their facial hair grow, were destined not to have land, and had no chance of marriage.

• Although in modern Japan the type of discrimination represented in the words like ズンム (zunmu) and やっこ (yakko) has long since disappeared, I cannot say for certain if the underlying mindset has completely vanished. In the back country of Japan, where old traditions continue to have a strong hold, first sons still tend to be treated more favorably than the rest, even if it's not to the degree it used to be.

Commentary:

• In Japan, it's still not so uncommon for parents to live with their first son and his wife. Relationship issues that arise between in-laws are something that many Japanese experience on some level—especially if they're in this situation.

• Mr. Leftover Pee is sitting on a typical 縁側 (engawa) that faces the yard of a traditional Japanese house. 縁側 (engawa) is a sort of plank placed right outside of the regular rooms. It functions like a porch or a veranda of a western style house.

責め地獄

TORTURE HELL

Zunmu 1: Gu he he he he. You got caught quite easily, Kamui.

Kamui: Please don't!

Zunmu 1: There, there! The tickle torture!

Kamui: No, don't♥

Zunmu 1: Oh dear, we're on fire because of her.

Zunmu 2: What shall we do next for our pleasure . . .?

Zunmu 3: I told you to beat her up!!

FX: (zun) *A loud kick.*

その後の残尿課長2

LEFTOVER PEE SECTION CHIEF AFTERWARDS 2

Text: Leftover Pee Section Chief has reached his retirement.

Chief: Hm?

Chief: Ooh oh ohhhh

Chief: Oh oh oooh

Woman: Oh dear, how nice . . .
Kid 1: Kyah
Chief: You wait!
Kid 2: Kyah
Kid 3: Kyah
Text: Apparently, the townsfolk loved him . . .

Commentary:

• This is another one of the Kamui & Zunmu series. As I mentioned earlier, the ズンム (zunmu) had to lead a grim life with a harsh social status. The author's Kamui & Zunmu series pokes fun at the sexual frustrations many ズンム (zunmu) must have endured.

• The Ninja/Samurai who attacks ズンム (zunmu) in panel #4 is the same one who sent the ズンム (zunmu) after Kamui as assassins—this storyline is just about the only part that has any resemblance to the original カムイ伝 (kamui den).

Commentary:

• Apparently the kids are teasing him and making him upset, while the mothers think they're playing together nicely.

• The author continues to show that the old man's troubled retirement never ends. It's also clear that no one seems to understand how the old man is suffering...

龍の伝説

LEGEND OF A DRAGON

FX: (kapoon, kapoon) *A high-pitched, reverberating sound.*

Boy: Oh . . . A person whose head is missing.

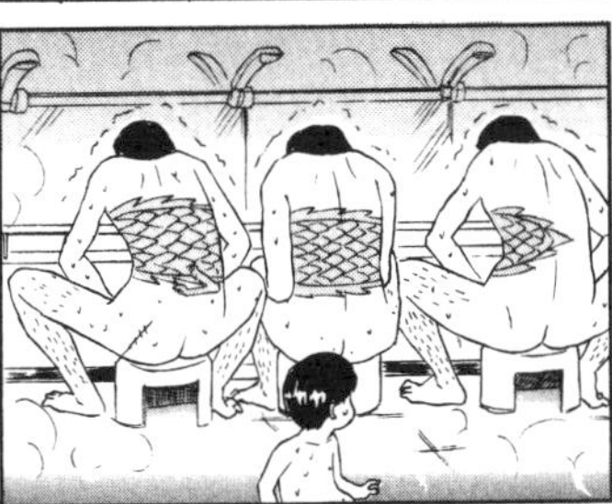

Text: The End

Commentary:

• This scene takes place in a public bathhouse. If you're lucky, you might encounter Yakuza with magnificent tattoos on them at a public bathhouse, and then, you'll realize that only a kid without any sense of fear can make a comment like the one above.

• Here is a picture of a typical public bathhouse:

残尿刑事

DETECTIVE LEFTOVER PEE

おっと動くなヨ
どてっ腹に
風穴あくぜ!!

Man: Hey, don't move! Unless you wanna get a bullet hole in your stomach!!

Detective: Hm?

FX: (chibibi) *The sound of the leak.*

Detective: Ooh oh!! Ooooh!!

Man: I told you not to move!!

Commentary:

• Nature's call cannot be controlled, and it sometimes happens at the most awkward moments. If you're someone who can't control your bladder that well (due to old age), a situation like this could really be troublesome...

しんばん まさきちせいだん
新版 政吉政談

NEW—MASAKICHI POLITICAL TALK

Woman: Striped mosquitoes' season's here.

Boss: Can't be helped. Ha ha ha . . .

Woman: Arrgh, it's so itchy.

Woman: They even bit me over here.

Man: Boss, did anything good happen to you or what?

Boss: Ahem—No, nothing.

Text: Masakichi thanked God for what happened that day—The End.

Commentary:

• As I mentioned earlier, the slang パンチラ (panchira) has a special meaning. パン (pan) is short for panties and チラ (chira) comes from ちらり (chirari), which means "to catch a glimpse of." As the existence of the slang itself suggests, パンチラ (panchira) is a popular fetish for Japanese men...

• And yes, the パンチラ (panchira) fetish can take many forms.

せんせい ひみつ
先生の秘密2

DOCTOR'S SECRET 2

Doctor: Sorry to make you come over, but, in fact . . .

Nurse: What is it, sir?

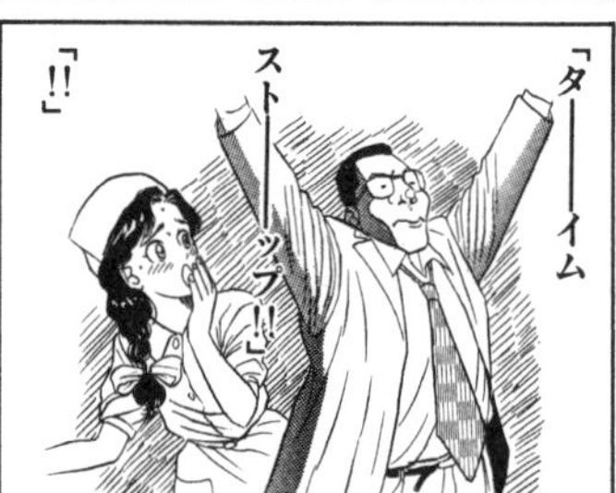

Doctor: Time!!
Doctor: Stop!!
Nurse: !!

Doctor: It's pink today . . .

Text: The doctor who anticipated white was disappointed—The End

Boy 1: It's every man's dream!!

Boy 2: I don't know, but it's pretty hip.

Commentary:

• Here's another one of the ビニ本 (bini hon) series. As I mentioned, ビニ本 (bini hon) is the plastic covered magazine sold through vending machines in 1970s. This genre of magazine is currently called エロ本 (erohon), which is the type of magazines that generally appeals to the carnal desires of the male population. They are now sold without plastic covers.

シリーズ
川島日記(かわしまにっき)

朝(あさ)の詩(うた)
ウチの前(まえ)で
悠然(ゆうぜん)と
糞(くそ)をたれる
近所(きんじょ)のガキ

Series
Kawashima's Diary

From right: Morning Ballad

In front of my house

Calmly

Shitting

Neighbor's tyke

Commentary:

• If you thought it was funny, you get the author's sense of humor. If not, don't worry.

はんば　はな
飯場の花4

FLOWER OF THE CONSTRUCTION CAMP 4

Song: Chan chan cha lan lalan lan lan

FX: (puri puri) *Sexy hip swing.*

Song: Chan chan cha lan lalan lan lan

FX: (puri puri) *Sexy hip swing.*

Girl: Everyone, good morning.♥

Girl: It's time to get up.♥

Man: Will you stop it, Hana-chan?

FX: (kin kin kin kin . . .) *Hard-on, hard-on, hard-on, hard-on . . .*

Commentary:

• 飯場 (hanba) is a type of temporary camp, where construction workers or miners live while on the job. Workers tend to sleep on typical Japanese futon bedding, laid out on a 畳 (tatami) mat floor .

TORTURE HELL

Text: Again, Kamui is pursued relentlessly—

Zunmu: (gu he he he he) *Sleazy snigger.*

Kamui: I won't let you beat me up like that all the time.

Kamui: Art of multiplication!!

Kamui: Oh no♥

Kamui: Oh no♥

PICTURE OF HELL

Woman: Kyaaah

FX: (go go go go) *An ominous grumble.*

Director: No good.

Man: The director, who's known for his supreme realism,

Man: will have to turn to special FX after all, huh?

FX: (zawa zawa zawa zawa) Noise of the agitated crowd.

Director: Don't you dare wear a bra!!

Commentary:

• 分身の術 (bunshin no jutsu) is a special technique that a Ninja uses to appear as if he/she has multiplied. This is done by creating phantoms that look exactly like him/her. This trick often appears in Samurai/Ninja type manga/anime.

• The logistics behind the 分身の術 (bunshin no jutsu) appear to vary. Some reason that the phantoms are visual illusions created by the super-fast moving Ninja—i.e., because the Ninja moves so fast, opponents see him/her in multiple places all at once. Others reason that they are created by the shadows of other objects. In this case, the Ninja makes his/her opponents believe that the shadows look exactly like him/her.

• 白土三平 (shirato sanpei), the author of カムイ伝 (kamui den), often uses the 分身の術 (bunshin no jutsu) in his stories. His version of 分身の術 (bunshin no jutsu) is, more or less, the one where a Ninja creates phantom images of himself/herself by moving super fast.

Commentary:

• 地獄変 (jigoku hen) is a short version of 地獄変相 (jigoku henso). 地獄 (jigoku) is Hell, and 変相 (henso) is, in this case, a picture that depicts either hell or heaven.

• Of course, the リアリズムの鬼 (riarizumu no oni) would not go for the special effects. Because of his unyielding style of realism, he can't even have an actress wear a bra.

• You may wonder which panel shows the true 地獄変 (jigoku hen)...

あいらぶゆー♡

「あら さっちゃん」
「あいらぶ ゆ～～～～♡」
「英語おぼえたの? さっちゃん」
「あいらぶ ゆ～～ッ♡」
「おりこうさんねェ ホホホホ…」
「あいらぶ ゆ～～～♡」
「ホホホ また明日ね さっちゃん…」
茂吉は
マジに うけとめた

I LOVE YOU

Woman 1: Oh, Sacchan.

Sacchan: I love you.

Woman 1: You've learned English, Sacchan?

Sacchan: I love you.

Woman 2: What a smart girl you are, ho ho ho ho . . .

Sacchan: I love you.

Woman 1: Ho ho ho, see you tomorrow, Sacchan . . .

Text: As for Mokichi . . .

Text: He took it to his heart—

Commentary:

• あいらぶゆー (ai rabu yu) is a Japanese phonetic way of spelling out "I love you." マジ (maji) is slang that means "being serious."

• Here is a picture of a classic street corner with the traditional-style walls. They're not so uncommon in Japan, even today:

先生

うりゃ うりゃ うりゃ～ッ
問題解くまで 帰さないわよ～～～～～ッ
おお～～っ
ドス バキッ ドド
あーゆー 先生に 習いたかった ですナァ…
まさに "光陰 矢の如し" ですなァ

SENSEI

Sensei: Urya, urya, uryaah!!

Sensei: I won't let you go home until you solve the problem.

Men: Ooh!!

FX: (dosu baki do) *A series of heavy blows and kicks.*

Man 1: I wish I learned from a teacher like her . . .

Man 2: "Time flies" indeed.

Commentary:

• 光陰 (kouin) means days, months and years. 矢 (ya) is the arrow. 光陰矢の如し (kouin yano gotoshi) is a Japanese phrase which means "time flies past as quickly as a shooting arrow." The meaning behind the phrase is not to waste away one's life idly—because time flies past.

• In modern society, a teacher like her would be considered abusive. If this happened in North American schools, for instance, she'd be sued by the parents. How different it was a couple of generations ago...

無償の愛 UNREQUITED LOVE

Husband: Oh goodness, how sweaty she is!!

Husband: I'd better change her right away!!

Husband: Hm!?

Husband: I didn't know that the panties were . . .

Husband: double layered here!!

Husband: Hmmm

Husband: It's not the time to do that right now!!

Husband: Gotta change her! Gotta change her!!

Commentary:

• The author is making fun of some men's eternal fascination with female panties. After all, even when his wife is lethargic, due to a high fever, he cannot help examining how the panties are structured. You can only imagine what went on both in his mind and in reality...

佐智子と美由紀 SACHIKO AND MIYUKI

Sachiko: Ahn!

Miyuki: Here, eat them all.

Miyuki: Oei said, "Not that one, please."

FX: (suu suu) *The steady, rhythmic sound of sleep—sound asleep.*

Husband: What's wrong, Sachiko? Did you wet your bed or something?

Sachiko: (kusun kusun) *Sobbing.*

Sachiko: I don't know why she doesn't call me "Oneh-san."

FX: (guu guu) Snoring.

Commentary:

• どうちて (douchite) is どうして (doushite = why) spoken in baby tongue.

• かちら (kachira) is かしら (kashira = I wonder) spoken in baby tongue.

• お義姉さん (oneh-san) means sister-in-law. Without the Kanji character 義, お姉さん (oneh-san) means sister, not the in-law. It's just that, お姉さん (oneh-san) means older sister, and Sachiko is hardly an older sister...

• Traditionally in Japan, babies sleep on a small futon bed beside their parents, like the one illustrated in this comic strip.

スケスケカルメン

SEE-THROUGH CARMEN

Man: Why do you bother to stay with me?

Man: Are you in love with me?

Woman: That's wrong . . .

Woman: It's you who's in love with me.

Text: See-Through Teacher thought that did the job.

Commentary:

• As you know, Carmen is the seductive, arrogant, and flirtatious gypsy prostitute, originally introduced in the 1845 novel by Prosper Mérimée. The charm of Carmen has given rise to ballets, plays and films, capturing the imagination of people around the world.

• In this comic strip, スケスケ先生 (suke suke sensei) is given a pompous slant. It's just that she has kept her innocent looks. This captures the man's heart. Remember, it's the sunny, sweet look that many Japanese guys wind up falling for.

彷徨

WANDERING

Girl A: What do you think of the visiting teachers?

Girl B: What? I don't like 'em.

Girl A: Nope. They're all old geezers.

Girl B: Yup I agree. I don't like blokes.

FX: (haa haa haa) Breathing hard.

Man A: I haven't seen something this good for a while.

Man B: It was worth coming all the way to Yamagata.

Commentary:

• The girls are talking in the heavy accent of the 東北 (tohoku) region of Japan. 東北 (tohoku) is the northern part of the main island of Japan.

• ござった (gozatta) is いらした (irashita) in 東北弁(tohoku-ben = Tohoku dialect), and it means "has come to visit." しぇんしぇー (shienshe) is 先生 (sensei) with the heavy accent. やんだ (yanda) is 嫌だ (iyada), which is an expression of one's distaste. んだなー (ndanah) is そうだね (soda-ne), which, in this case, means "I think so too."

• 山形 (yamagata) is one of the prefectures in the 東北 (tohoku) region.

• Here is a map of Japan with the 東北 (tohoku) region marked for your reference:

Tohuku

夕立ち

CAUGHT IN A SHOWER

Boss: It's raining hard.

Girl: How troublesome...

Girl: Look, my skirt is soaking wet.

FX: (zaa zaa) *The sound of pouring rain.*

Man 1: Ah? Are you crying, Boss?

Man 2: Did something good happen to you?

Commentary:

• Once again the male パンチラ (panchira) fetish is depicted here.

• As I mentioned earlier, the Japanese slang パンチラ (panchira) is key to understanding this. パン (pan) is short for panties and チラ (chira) comes from ちらり (chirari), which means "to catch a glimpse of." As the existence of the slang itself suggests, パンチラ (panchira) is a popular fetish for Japanese men. Also, the 親方 (oyakata = boss) truly appreciates the opportunity.

あれから10年たちました

IT'S BEEN TEN YEARS SINCE THEN

Girl: Oh no. Don't they bite? Don't they?

Boy: Don't worry about that...

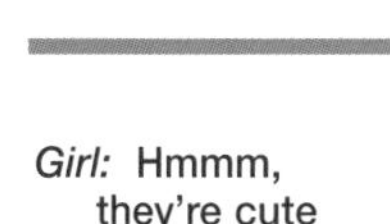

Girl: Hmmm, they're cute once I get used to them.

Boy: ...

Woman: Yoh, it's great to see you after such a long time.

Man: Oh, it's you.

Woman: So, how're you doing?

Man: She hasn't changed, has she?

Commentary:

• From the words spoken by the man in panel #3, we can tell they are not on a date. From their conversation and the title of this comic strip, it is apparent that the scenes in panel #3 and #4 are taking place at their class reunion.

• The class reunion is taking place in a classic 座敷 (zashiki) setting with the 畳 (tatami) mat, the straw mat flooring, and 座布団 (zabuton), the traditional square cushions, at a traditional Japanese restaurant.

•Here's what typical 座敷 (zashiki) room looks like at a traditional Japanese restaurant:

私は貝になりたい

I WANT TO BE A SHELLFISH

Man: You're chatting too loud in front of my house!!

FX: (baan) *A loud bang.*

Sachiko: I'm so sorry...

Sachiko: (euuu) *Crying.*

Echoing: I'm so sorry.
I'm so sorry.
I'm so sorry.
I'm so sorry.
I'm so sorry.
I'm so sorry.

Man: Arrgh... What have I done?

Commentary:

• Even this fierce-looking man feels guilty after yelling at the little girl. That soft spot in him is what makes us like him. And, the gag—the man wants to be a shellfish so that he can hide away (perhaps from his guilty feelings). If you find this funny, you really share the author's sense of humor.

刺繍

EMBROIDERY

Girl: It's getting hot and humid.

Text: Strip.

Girl: If it's like this everyday, I can't take it.

Masakichi: ...

Text: Flower

Girl: This? It's the one-point embroidery.

Girl: Will you keep this a secret from the others?

Text: That night—

Text: Masakichi worked on embroidering his underwear.

Commentary:

• The Kanji character embroidered on the girl's underwear, 花 (hana), means flower. It means that the girl's name must be 花 (hana). The characters in this comic strip and the setting also suggest that this is another one of the "Flower of The Construction Camp" series.

• 政吉 (masakichi) is the boss at the construction camp.

• It may appear silly to see 政吉 (masakichi) embroidering (probably his name) onto his underwear. The psychology behind his actions is his excitement over sharing a secret with the girl. It's almost a kid-like sensibility, but that's why he is so endearing.

5時20分

5:20

Man: Good evening. It's time for Shoten.

Man: We're entering the rainy season soon...

Girl: (kukaka) Making noise in her sleep.

Man: Frogs sing from over here.

Girl: (ngagaga kukaka...) *Making noise in her sleep.*

Man: And, they sing from over there.

Man: We have Koji and Kyuji, the Aozora brothers, the comedians you all know!

FX: (pachi pachi pachi...) Clapping hands.

Man: Let's get started in high spirits!!

Commentary:

• 笑点 (shoten) is a popular TV show that first appeared in 1966, and it has aired over 1,900 episodes. It continues to air every week, entertaining Japanese viewers with its celebrated comedians.

• 青空球児 & 好児 (aozora kyuji & koji) are comedians. They are not brothers by birth. Their partnership as comedians started in 1966. ゲーロゲロ (gehro gero) is one of their best-known gags, which brought them to stardom.

• The camera man couldn't help focusing on the girl with her panties showing. Oops, she's on-air across Japan...

さちことみゆき2

SACHIKO AND MIYUKI 2

Mother: C'mon, greet your Oneh-san!!

Miyuki: Yeah...

Miyuki: H—Hello...

Sachiko: How d'you do?

Sachiko: (kusun kusun) Sobbing.

Miyuki: ...

Miyuki: She's like a little kid...

Commentary:

• お義姉さん (oneh-san) means sister-in-law. Without the Kanji character 義, お姉さん (oneh-san) means sister, not the in-law.

• Many Japanese couples nowadays choose to have a Western-style wedding. It is also common for couples to have a Western-style reception, followed by a traditional Japanese-style ceremony. In this case, the newly married couples will have the opportunity to dress in both traditional Japanese and Western-style garments during the wedding.

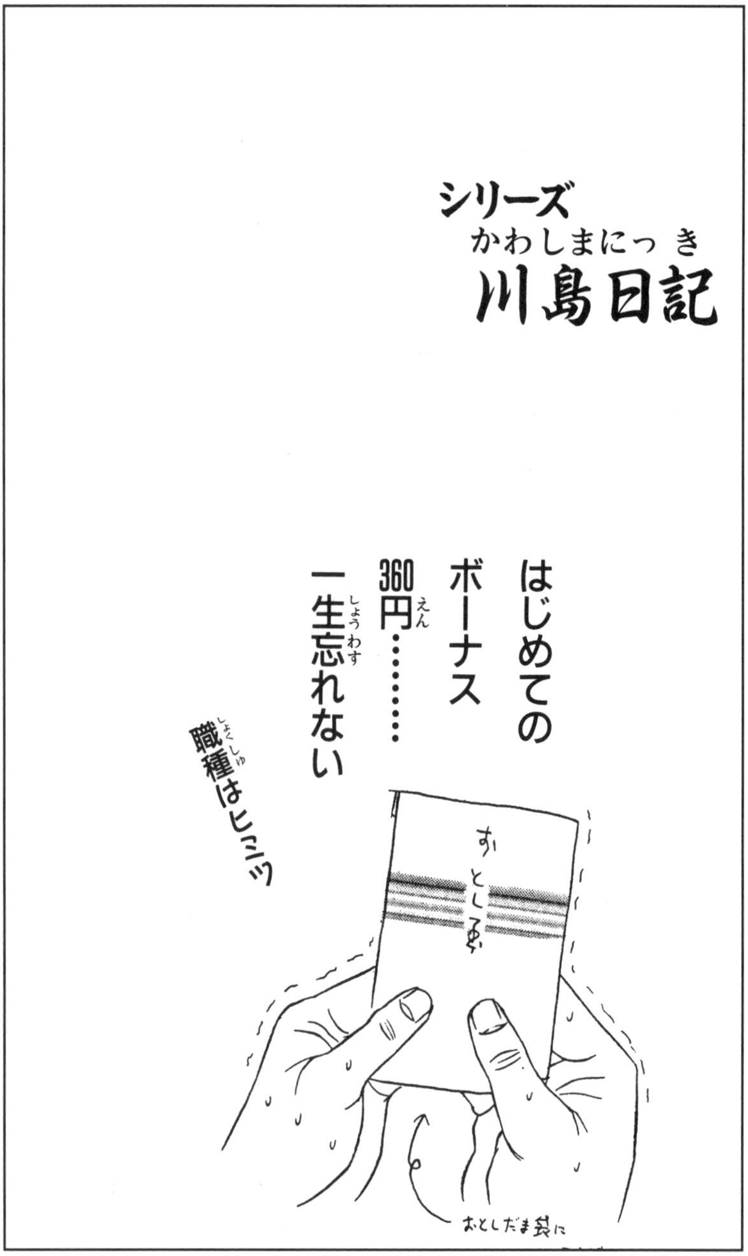

シリーズ
かわしまにっき
川島日記

Series Kawashima's Diary

はじめての
ボーナス
360円(えん)……
一生忘(しょうわす)れない

職種(しょくしゅ)はヒミツ

おとし玉

おとしだま袋に

Right: The first bonus I received was 360 yen... I'll never forget that.

Slanted text: The employer is a secret.

Text on the envelope: Otoshidama

Text with an arrow: It came in an Otoshidama envelope.

Commentary:

• The value of 360 yen is rather hard to judge. From 1949 through 1971, the exchange rate was fixed, and one US dollar could buy 360 yen. In the early 1980s, it could buy 200 plus yen. But, nowadays, it can only buy a little over 100 yen. Nonetheless, in the 1970s, 360 yen could buy a lot more than what it can today. For instance, in 1970, it cost about 700 yen to buy a movie ticket, while today it costs almost 3,000 yen. Public bathhouses charged about 40 yen in 1970, while now they charge around 400 yen.

• It is a Japanese tradition to give the gift of money on the New Year's Day. This is called おとし玉 (otoshidama). The giver of the おとし玉 (otoshidama) usually places money inside an envelop designed specifically for おとし玉 (otoshidama). It's typical for grandparents, parents, uncles, aunts and sometimes family friends, to give おとし玉 (otoshidama) to their kids. Once a kid starts earning money, though, he/she is likely to give おとし玉 (otoshidama) to his/her or someone else's kids.

情念の炎

FIRE OF PASSION

Monster: Are you alright, miss?

Woman: M—My heart aches...

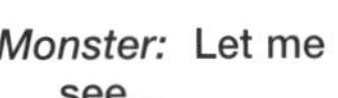

Monster: Let me see...

FX: (doun) *A loud explosion.*

Monster: This is her new trick, huh?

Monster 1: It certainly is a fire play—with her life on the line.

Monster 2: Having Etsuko Shihomi as our partner lights me on fire!!

乳房

BOSOMS

Sachiko: Hmm... Boobies!

Miyuki: Oh no, don't touch, Oneh-san.

Sachiko: Mmmm... Mama...

FX: (chuba chuba) *Sucking sound.*

Miyuki: ...

Miyuki: ...

FX: (kapoon) *A high-pitched, reverberating sound.*

FX: (chuba chuba) *Sucking sound.*

Man: It—It makes me cry.

Old Man: My tears blur my vision...

Commentary:

• 志保美悦子 (shihomi etsuko) is an actress who appeared in many action films in 1970s and 80s. With her well-known athletic ability, she was able to carry out many amazing stunts on her own. She is also known as Sue Shiomi in North America. She married a popular singer 長渕剛 (nagabuchi tsuyoshi) in 1987 and left her acting career behind.

• Apparently, the author brought 志保美悦子 (shihomi etsuko) into his ももレンジャー (momo renjaa = Pink Ranger) series to make a special appearance.

• Here are some of the movie titles with 志保美悦子 (shihomi etsuko): Killing Machine; Dragon Princess; Samurai Reincarnation; Karate Warriors; Street Fighter; Legend of the Eight Samurai; Return of the Street Fighter; The Bodyguard; Shogun's Samurai.

Commentary:

• Miyuki and Sachiko are taking a bath together in a typical Japanese bathtub. As you may have deduced from the wide-spread public bathhouses in Japan, it's not uncommon for same sex persons to take a bath together in Japan. Unlike western style bathing, most Japanese households have one bathtub in separate bathing room. The bathtub is prepared with warm (or rather hot) water. Taking turns, everyone in the household uses the same water—and some may share the bathtub together. If you're not the last person taking a bath, it's impolite to use up all the water, and you'd better not drain the bathtub without asking.

• Of course, it's the author's sense of humor to twist the scene so that Sachiko, the sister-in-law, ends up sucking Miyuki's breast.

南国の対決

CONFRONTATION IN SOUTHERN COUNTRY

Tama-chan: Urrgh, it's itchy along the panty line.

FX: (hori hori) *Scratching sound.*

Girl 1: Will you stop it, Tama-chan.

Tama-chan: Hmmm

Girl 2: Someone might be watching, you know.

Girl 1: They're still here today!

Girl 2: Can't stand them. Don't peek! Don't!

Man 1: ...It was great...

Man 2: I'm glad we came all the way to Kokura...

Commentary:

• 小倉 (Kokura) is located in 福岡 (Fukuoka) prefecture inside the 北九州市 (Kita-kyushu-shi), which is located in the 九州 (Kyushu) region. It appears that the middle-aged Three Musketeers have continued on with their wandering and made their way down. From the look of it, their mission is to peek inside the girl's locker room.

さっちゃん のり弁

SACCHAN'S SEAWEED LUNCH

Sachiko: Miyuki-tan, you've left your lunch behind.

FX: (haa haa) *Huffing hard.*

Miyuki: Wow, thanks, Neh-san.

Miyuki: Don't bother to come by for god's sake!

Sachiko: E he heh...

FX: (guu) *Grumbling stomach.*

Miyuki: ....

Miyuki: ... Here! Ahn!

Sachiko: Ahn.

Commentary:

• The suffix たん (tan) that follows directly after a person's name, such as Miyuki-tan, is a cute, infant's way of pronouncing さん (san).

• えへへー (e he heh), in this instance, is a timid giggle.

• From the drawing of the desks and chairs, it is clear that Miyuki is at school. The girls are wearing school uniforms, and the school is probably a girls-only high school (because I don't see any boys in the picture.) There are still public high schools in Japan that admit boys only or girls only. Usually, if there's a girls-only high school in town, it's likely that a boys-only high school will also exist in the same town.

おやつですよ

SNACK TIME

FX: (kote kote) *Dipping.*

Miyuki: Kuma-san, it's time for a snack!

Miyuki: Grrrr!

FX: (pero pero) *Licking.*

Text: Honey

Miyuki: Hey, don't drip...

FX: (pero pero) *Licking.*

Miyuki: I don't know if my life should be spent like this...

FX: (pero pero) *Licking.*

Text: Honey

Commentary:

• くま (kuma) is a bear. Thus, くまさん (kuma-san) is equivalent to Ms. Bear.

• You might have noticed by now that Sachiko lives in a small Japanese home with a traditional 畳 (tatami) mat floor. They're playing in a typical 茶の間 (chanoma), where the family eats its meals. It also functions as a family room.

シリーズ
かわしまにっき
川島日記

Series
Kawashima's Diary

ウインクすると
値引くと
思われていた
らしい……
ばちっ
ばちっ
にこごり
小女子

FX: (bachi bachi) *series of hard winks*

Text: I guess customers thought they'd get discounts if they winked....

Text: Nikogori

Text: Kounago

Commentary:

• にこごり (nikogori) is a type of congealed food made with gelatinous fish-like sea breams and flatfish. 小女子 (kounago) is a type of small fish perfect for a tempura dish.

• This is obviously based on the actual experience of the author when he was a fishmonger. Please note the way he's dressed. It's the typical outfit worn by fishmongers.

• Here's a picture of how a typical fishmonger dresses:

花の降る午後 — FLOWERING AFTERNOON

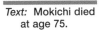

Sachiko: Ojii-chan, my next door neighbor.

Old Man: Oh, Sacchan.

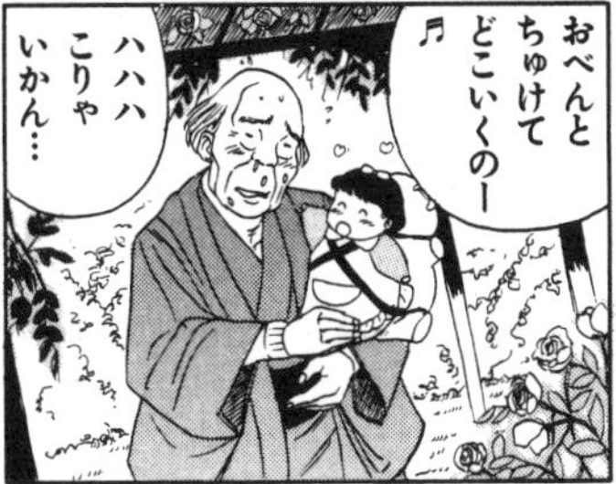

Song: Where're you going with your lunch on your face.

Old Man: Ha ha ha, that's not good...

Sachiko: E he he...

FX: (pero) *Lick.*

FX: (gaan) *An expression indicating that he is stunned and feels as if a rock has been dropped on his head.*

Text: Mokichi died at age 75.

Text: I hear he had no regrets.

青春キャンパス — SEISHUN CAMPUS

Girl: Tome-chan, you're not wearing the underskirt?

Tome-chan: I don't like that stuffy feeling, you know.

Tome-chan: Please don't tell anyone about this, will you?

Girl: I'm not wearing it either.

Girls: Ho ho ho

Man 1: It's great that they're magnanimous here in Kyoto...

Man 2: I'd love to die on this land...

Commentary:

• You may not quite understand what's going on here. If so, take a closer look, and you'll notice there are several grains of cooked rice on the old man's face. That's why Sachiko sings "where're you going with your lunch on your face." With a timid giggle, she licks his face to taste the rice—and the old man has a heart-attack, which leads to his death. You might recall (from the previous comic strip involving this old man) how he was in love with Sachiko...

• Please note that Sachiko has a stuffed bear on her back. What she's doing is mimicking mothers who carry their babies on their back.

• Although nowadays many mothers carry their babies in front, like people tend to do in Western countries, traditionally Japanese mothers have carried their babies on their backs.

Commentary:

• The middle-aged Three Musketeers are now visiting 京都 (Kyoto) where temples and exotic sights from the good-old-days in Japan still abound. And, of course, they have to seek out the girls in tennis outfits.

• You must understand the fact that female tennis outfits are something Japanese men tend to love—at least the type of men whom the author is constantly making fun of. With a fetish for glimpsing the girls' panties, you know why tennis wear is so hot.

愛のさかあがり

FORWARD HIP CIRCLE WITH LOVE

Girl: Yah, yah, yah♥

FX: (bata bata) *Struggling.*

Girl: Masayoshi, push me!!

FX: (bata bata) *Struggling.*

Girl: Push my butt!!

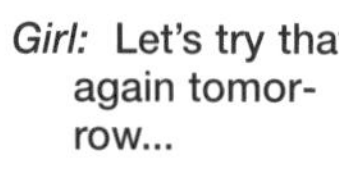

Girl: Did you get how to do the forward hip circle...?

Girl: (haa) *Huffing.*

Masayoshi: No, I didn't.

Girl: Let's try that again tomorrow...

Girl: (haa) *Deep sigh.*

Text: Masayoshi thought he wouldn't mind, even if he never learned how.—The End.

Commentary:

• わかっただか (wakatta-daka) is わかったか (wakatta-ka) with a heavy accent. It means something like, "Did you understand?"

• わがんね (wagan-ne) is わからない (wakara-nai) with a heavy accent. It means "I didn't understand."

• またやんべか (mata yanbeka) is またやろうか (mata yarouka) with a heavy accent. She's asking if he wants to try it again.

• The girl appears to be the boy's sister, but she could be someone who's not related to him. This comic strip shows that even the little boy can get turned on by girls. But the little boy has an advantage. The girl wouldn't have done this with someone older. The author's point might be that there are many men who'd love to be a boy again and appreciate these things.

流れる?

FORFEITED?

Man: Lad... You've lost it all already? Ha ha ha.

Young Man: Ku u u!!

Young Man: I'm not done yet. Let me do it!!

Young Man: Otherwise, it wasn't worth the trouble to have pawned my wife!

Text: Pawn Shop

Text: Pawn Shop

Man: How troublesome—

Commentary:

• くううっ (ku u u) is a growling sort of sound, and in this instance, it shows the young man's frustration at being in a tight spot or beaten.

• The clothing that the young man is wearing (see panel #2) is a classic, casual outfit for men. It inspires the image of a not-so-modern, blue-collar worker.

男の世界ダ

IT'S A MAN'S WORLD

Fat boy: Is that you who's transferred schools from Tokyo?

Boy: So what?

Fat boy: Humph, Kankoh, huh? It's so not cool!

Fat boy: Mine's Benkugah!!

Fat boy: Do you know what Benkuga is?

Fat boy: If you got that, stop acting so stuck up.

旅の終わり

END OF THE JOURNEY

Text: Please tie your shoestrings here.

Girl: My school comes up with the stupidest rules.

Men: Oooh!

おわり

Man 1: After all, Osaka gave us the final blow!!

Man 2: It's great that they're so willing to be open!!

Outside the panel: The End

Commentary:

• The fat boy is speaking with a heavy accent. おめか (omeka) is おまえか (omaeka), which means "Is that you?" だっしぇーなぁ (dassheh-nah) is だざいなぁ (dasai-nah), which means "It's so not cool." わがっだら (wagaddara) is わかったら (wakattara), which means "If you get that."

• カンコー (kankoh) and ベンクーガー (benkugah) are brands of school uniforms.

• I think this is a parody of human nature. Somehow, what you wear defines who you are. Oh well, it's unfortunate, but isn't that how people often feel? Sometimes, you just can't fight it.

Commentary:

• ガッコ (gakko) is a colloquial and casual way of saying 学校 (gakkō), which means school. 作らへんな (tsukura-henna) is 作らないな (tsukura-naina) with an Osaka accent.

• The middle-aged Three Musketeers have traveled around Japan from the North to the South, and their journey appears to be coming to an end in Osaka. The point is, no matter where they are, so long as they can catch a glimpse of girls' panties or bras, they're happy. Call them what you will, you now know how little it takes for middle-aged men to be happy.

MONROE WALK

Girl: Going to the ocean on a pair of high-heeled sandals...

FX: (puriri) *Sexy hip swing.*

Girl: Doing that Monroe Walk.

FX: (puri puri) *Sexy hip swing.*

Man: Hey, it's hot.

FX: (karan) *Rattle.*

Man: Morning service, please.

Girl: It's already over. I'm so sorry!

FX: (gaku) *Disappointed.*

Man: Arrgh!

Commentary:

• There is a song called "Monroe Walk" by 南佳孝 (minami yoshitaka) released in 2001, and the girl is singing that song.

• "Monroe Walk" has become a term in Japan that means "a girl's way of walking with that sexy hip swing." Of course, "Monroe" refers to Marilyn Monroe with her famous sex appeal. Remember how she walked?

• Also note that the term "Monroe Walk" is used as the name for numerous bars in Japan.

• What's funny is that the man is asking for "morning service." How many bars in North America would be this crowded in the morning, with guys drinking and looking at sexy girls?

シリーズ

かわしまにっき
川島日記

1991　就職

「おまえはもう
人間じゃない
今日から
機械に
なるンだ!!」

職種はヒミツ

Series
Kawashima's Diary

Horizontal Text: 1991 Got a new job

Vertical Text: "You're no longer a man. As of today, you are a machine!!"

Slanted Text: The type of employment is a secret.

Commentary:

- Well, we can't help but wonder what kind of job this is...

修学旅行の朝 (しゅうがくりょこう あさ)

MORNING OF SHUGAKU-RYOKO

Miyuki: Bye, I'm going!

FX: (tat tat tat) Rushing away.

Miyuki: I'm late! I'm late!

Sachiko: Miyuki, please wait!

Miyuki: I gotta go!! What is it?!

Sachiko: S— Some pocket money for you.

FX: (jara) *Sound of the coins.*

Miyuki: ...

Sachiko: You'll be really late, Miyuki.

FX: (gusun) *A snuffing sound, indicating that tears are welling up.*

Miyuki: Yup... Hehe...

Commentary:

• 修学旅行 (shugaku ryoko) is a common school event in Japan in which students go on an excursion for educational purposes. It usually takes place once a year, and older students go on 修学旅行 (shugaku ryoko) instead of 遠足 (ensoku). Unlike 遠足 (ensoku), which is an all day event, 修学旅行 (shugaku ryoko) involves an overnight stay—sometimes more than one night. 修学 (shugaku) means " to study and learn." 旅行 (ryoko) means "trip."

• Students often bring their allowances to purchase items at the destination as a keepsake or as gifts.

• へへ (hehe) in panel #4 is a shy giggle, which is more or less made to hide her tears.

卵 (たまご)

EGGS

Girl: Oh no, why are there eggs here?

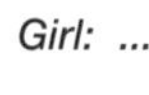

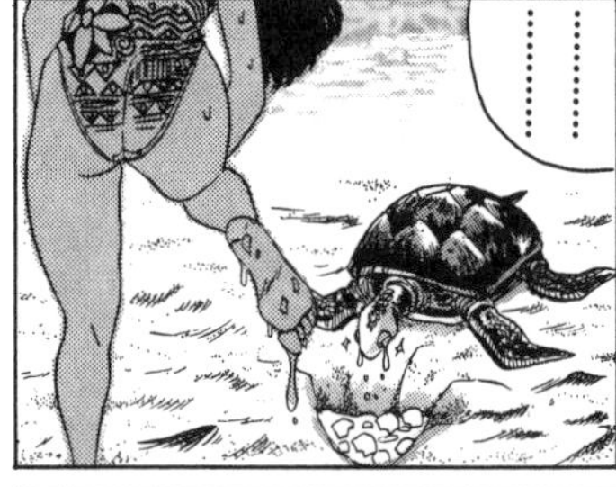

Girl: ...

Turtle: (shiku shiku shiku shiku) Sobbing.

Girl: I'm so sorry.

FX: (zaa zazaa) *Sound of the wave.*

Commentary:

• It is a fact that humans have significantly reduced the population of sea turtles. The damaging activities include capturing the turtles, harvesting the eggs, altering and destroying the nesting beaches, polluting the ocean, and snaring the turtles in fish/shrimp nets.

• Sea turtles make lengthy migrations from hatching beaches to feeding grounds and back again. Pacific loggerhead sea turtles, for example, hatch on Japanese beaches and then swim all the way to their feeding grounds off Baja California. Because of this migration process, they are faced with many threats along the way, and you can understand why they are now an endangered species.

• Let's hope none of us will experience what the girl has done in this comic strip.

嗚呼!! 絶好球

AH!! GREAT BALL

FX: (basun) *A loud thud.*

Someone: Ah, great ball.

Someone: Passing this great ball?

FX: (dosun) *A loud thud.*

Someone: Tut, this makes it three-strikes...

FX: (basun) *A loud thud.*

Someone: Ouch—Ouch—

FX: (basu dosu baki dosu) *A series of hard kicks.*

Someone: Stop it! You, polka dots!

Commentary:

• 水玉 (mizutama) means "polka dots." But in this case, he's referring to the girl who's wearing panties with a polka-dotted pattern.

• I wouldn't say that Japanese girls would never play baseball in skirts, but still, I believe this is more of the author's fantasy than reality in Japan.

• Also note that the girls can be quite violent—none of those sweet, submissive Japanese-girl stereotypes here.

着衣と裸体

DRESSED AND NAKED BODY

Student 1: She's not see-through today...

Student 2: Just wait a bit.

Student 2: Make a rectangle like this.

Student 2: And change the angle...

FX: (pa) *Flash.*

Student 2: It's her special effect.

Student 2: She knows how boys feel.

Commentary:

• This typifies the Japanese men's sentiment that nudity is more exciting when it's not fully revealed (i.e. when it's impossible to see everything).

• The word 男心 (otoko gokoro) represents the generally understood sentiment of men. 男 (otoko) means "man or male." 心 (kokoro) means "heart." 男心 (otoko gokoro) is a sentiment commonly shared by men which women would not feel. Similarly, with the Kanji character 女 (onna = woman or female), the word 女心 (onna gokoro) represents a women's sentiment. These words are all about how men and women feel differently and how different things attract them.

聞いてんのか川藤!

ARE YOU LISTENING, KAWATO?

Teacher: Because I care about you, I'm telling you this!!

Teacher: Are you listening, Kawato?

Girl 1: It's so hot.

Teacher: I believe in your potential!! Do you understand?

Teacher: Are you listening, Kawato?

Girl 1: It's so hot.

Girl 2: Yeah.

Commentary:

• There is a professional baseball player named 川藤 (kawato). The author might have named this character after him.

• Nonetheless, this is most likely another one of the パンチラ (panchira) gag series. So the boy, 川藤 (kawato), must have some talent—his talent could be in baseball—who knows. But it's just that he can't help focusing on the girls' panties—like so many boys with a fetish for パンチラ (panchira).

噂の真相

TRUTH BEHIND THE RUMOR

Interviewer 1: Sekitori, how's your condition?

Interviewer 2: What's your ambition this time?

Sachiko: (haa haa) Huffing.

Sachiko: Can you see your own weenie?

Sekitori: ...

Interviewer 1: Who are you going out with right now?

Interviewer 2: What type of woman?

Interviewer 3: What about the rumor about a love-child?

Sachiko: Can you see your own weenie?

Text: I heard that he left after he whispered "I can see it" in an almost inaudible voice.

Sachiko: Thanks...

Commentary:

• Sumo is one of Japan's national sports. Just like professional baseball in America, there are six divisions within professional Sumo leagues. The upper league is 幕内 (makunouchi), the middle league is 十両 (juryo), and the lower leagues are 幕下 (makushita), 三段目 (sandanme), 序二段 (jonidan), and 序の口 (jonokuchi).

• The Sumo wrestlers of 幕内 (makunouchi) and 十両 (juryo) are called 関取 (sekitori), and they receive salaries from the Sumo Association.

• The question Sachiko keeps asking is funny because it's something many Japanese people may have thought but never dared to express.

シリーズ
かわしまにっき
川島日記

ひ　や
日焼けすると
かお
顔がなくなるやつ

Series
Kawashima's Diary

Text: When I get suntanned, my face disappears.

Commentary:

• The author is making fun of his own face.

水の中の欲望 (みず なか よくぼう)

LUST UNDERWATER

FX: (kyoro kyoro) Looking around, searching.

FX: (sara sara) *The sound of peacefully flowing water.*

Zunmu: I'm glad I became shinobi . . .

Zunmu: I'm glad I became shinobi . . .

Zunmu: (gyaaaah) A shriek of pain.

FX: (doka ki baki gasu) A series of hard kicks/punches/stabs.

Commentary:

• 忍 (shinobi) is someone who secretly investigates, schemes, and assassinates, using the art of 忍術 ninjutsu). 忍 (shinobi) is more broadly known as 忍者 (ninja) due to the Ninja novels of the 1960s written by Huutarou Yamada. He called the professional assassins 忍者 (ninja) and the art of しのび (忍, shinobi) 忍法 (ninpou). The term he created went on to become the standard usage.

• During the 戦国時代 (sengoku jidai), which translates into the "era of civil war," 忍 (shinobi) worked successfully for different military factions in Japan. 忍 (shinobi) is also called 隠密 (onnmitsu), as well as 忍者 (ninja). Although there are various theories and opinions, in generally, the period from 1467 to 1615 is considered the 戦国時代 (sengoku jidai).

美容室

びようしつ

BEAUTY PARLOR

FX: (karo karo karo) *A rattling sort of sound made by the act of mixing.*

Man: . . .

Girl: No—

Girl: No!!!

FX: (sori sori...) *An expression indicating that he is shaving her.*

Commentary:

• やーん (yaan) is a feminine way of saying "oh, no!" or "no, don't!" It can sound quite coquettish, and of course, Japanese men tend to find it sexy.

• So, use your imagination and draw your own conclusions.

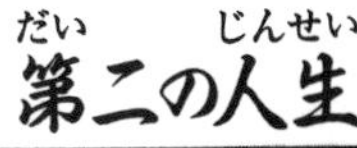

THE SECOND LIFE

FX: (puri puri) Sexy hip swing.

Girl: Excuse me. Would you hook my bra, please?

Girls: (kyaa kyaa) *Female scream of delight.*

Girl: Thanks a lot, Oji-san!

Girls: (kyahahaha-hahahahaha...) Female scream of delight.

FX: (sosokusa) *Hurries away.*

Man 1: What an unexpected harvest!

Man 2: I have no regrets with the second stage of my life.

Commentary:

• The Three Musketeers return. With this comic strip called "The Second Life," you may wonder if they've retired from teaching at this point. Perhaps they're no longer middle-aged men, but rather, dirty old men...

• Please note how the men are wearing fieldworkers' outfits and carrying baskets on their backs. They're supposedly harvesting something—it's just that, perhaps, they don't need the baskets if what they really want is to get another glimpse of the girls in the locker rooms.

①杏子

けものみち

きょうは だんなの まえの おくさんに あいました

ついに始まってしまった!! 連載マンガ"けものみち"!!

(1) YOKO Title: Animal Trail

Vertical text with an arrow: Finally, it's started!! A manga series called "Animal Trail!!"

Text: Today, I met with my hubby's ex-wife.

Handwritten: Husband

Handwritten: X-wife

Handwritten: Daughter

Husband: Yoko's grown a lot.

X-wife: She's eight this year.

FX: (tsuun) *Looks away—not friendly at all.*

Sachiko: . . .

Yoko: . . .

FX: (jii) *Staring hard.*

Sachiko: No

FX: (zun zun) *Poking*

Yoko: . . .

Commentary:

• けものみち (kemono michi), which translates to "animal trail," is the original series the author started with this comic strip. The main characters from his less cohesive series おさな妻 (oasanazuma) are further developed in this series and additional characters have been added. Also note, Sachiko, a.k.a. Sacchan, has gotten even younger than before...

②予感がする

きみたちアイスでもたべといで

ボクたちお話があるンダョ

(2) HAVING A PREMONITION

Husband: Why don't you guys go and have some ice cream?

Husband: We've got something to discuss between ourselves.

Miyuki: I have a bad feeling . . .

Text: I heard Miyuki felt it then.

FX: (bero bero bero) *Licking hard.*

Yoko: I'm not sharing this.

FX: (gaan) *An expression indicating that she's shocked and feels as if a rock has been dropped on her head.*

FX: (pui) *Looks away—not friendly at all.*

Commentary:

• As you might recall, Miyuki is Sacchan's sister-in-law.

③きいてくだちゃい

(3) WILL YOU LISTEN?

Sachiko: Hello, is this Monta Mino-tan?

Sachiko: I'm Sacchan.

Sachiko: Lately, my husband's so cold towards me.

Sachiko: What am I supposed to do? Ahn an ahn an.

Text: Please wait a moment.

— OO TV—

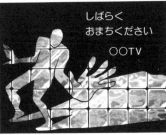

Sachiko: No one understands me.

Text: Sachiko felt lonely.

④さっちゃん はちみつ

(4) SACCHAN HONEY

Text: My hubby ran off with his ex-wife.

FX: (pero pero) *Licking sound.*

Text: Honey

Text: Honey

Sacchan: (euu) Crying.

Miyuki: Don't give up, Oneh-san . . .

Text below the panel: To Be Continued

Commentary:

• There's a TV show called 午後はＯＯおもいッきりテレビ (gogo wa marumaru omoikkiri terebi), which has become one of the staple, mid-day TV programs in Japan. みなもんた (mino monta) is the face of the show, and his appeal to housewives is known to be very powerful. It's rumored that the products he recommends on-air disappear from stores within a couple of days—apparently, housewives run out and buy out the stores.

• In the show, there's a segment where みなもんた (mino monta) takes calls from viewers and provides advice. Obviously, this comic strip is a parody of that show.

Commentary:

• I don't think the author is intending to portray a lesbian relationship here. Instead, I believe this is an intimate moment the author captured—perhaps because it's part of a fantasy some Japanese men might have.

シリーズ
かわしまにっき
川島日記

6月×日
とうとう
檀ふみの
ポスターを
手に入れた

Series
Kawashima's Diary

Text: Xth day of June. I finally got a hold of a poster that showed Fumi Dan.

Commentary:

• 檀ふみ (dan fumi) is a well-known actress and writer. She began her career as an actress in early 1970s while she was still a high school student. She has appeared in numerous films and TV shows and published many books.

30年後 (ねんご)

30 YEARS LATER

なあ
のぶちゃん
なアに?

Girl: Hey, Nobu-chan.

Nobuyo: What?

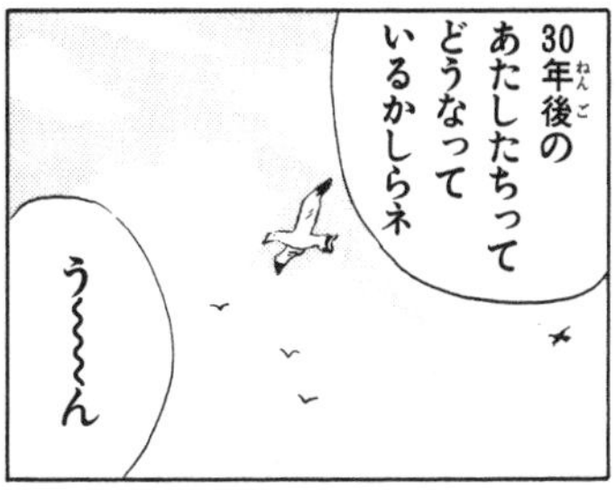
30年後のあたしたちってどうなっているかしらネ
う〜〜〜ん

Girl: I wonder what we'll be doing 30 years from now.

Nobuyo: Humph.

あたし絶対歌手になってるワ
ホホホ
がんばってね
のぶちゃん

Nobuyo: I'll become a professional singer no matter what.

Girl: Ho ho ho. Good luck, Nobu-chan.

大山のぶ代
18歳の
青春であった——
—完

Text: Nobuyo Ohyama.

Eighteen years old—it was her seishun then.

Girl: Ho ho ho ho . . .

Text: The End

Commentary:

• 大山のぶ代 (ohyama nobuyo) is the famous voice of the imaginary character ドラえもん (doraemon). Her career evolved mainly as a voice actress, and in the late 1970s when the ドラえもん (doraemon) series was first made into an anime, she took on the job. She has been the voice of ドラえもん (doraemon) ever since.

• 青春 (seishun) is a word used to describe the period of adolescence. It's the period most consider the spring of life, and often, many inexperienced and innocent youths dream of their future. Whether 大山のぶ代 (ohyama nobuyo) actually dreamed of being a singer I can't say.

• Please note the uncanny likeness of ドラえもん (doraemon) illustrated as the clouds in the sky on panel #4.

⑤おさな母（はは）

(5) CHILD MOTHER

Text outside the panel: A manga series: Animal Trail

Boy 1: Yoko-chan, wait!

Boy 1: Your new mom has come to pick you up!

Boys: Ha ha ha

Boy 2: Ha ha ha, you stupid, fool!

FX: (da) Dashing away.

FX: (haa haa) Huffing hard.

Sachiko: Yoko-tan, wait!

Yoko: Don't follow me!

Text: Yoko couldn't become friends with her new mother.

⑥おさな母（はは）2

(6) CHILD MOTHER 2—

Text: Sachiko adopted Yoko, the child of her husband and his former wife.

FX: (suu suu) The steady, rhythmic sound of sleep—sound asleep

FX: (peto peto peto . . .) Dripping honey.

FX: (ngaga . . . nga) Making noise in her sleep.

Yoko: What're you doing? You fool!!!

FX: (pero pero) Licking honey.

Text: Sachiko wants to become friends with Yoko.

Yoko: Don't follow me!!

Text: But, Yoko wouldn't accept her.

Commentary:

• The boys and Yoko are carrying classic school backpacks. They are called ランドセル (randoseru), and almost all elementary school children buy them when they enter the 1st grade. They use these backpacks for six years. They tend to come in two colors: the red ones are for the girls and black ones are for the boys. Once the children graduate from elementary school, they also graduate from ランドセル (randoseru).

Commentary:

• And, no wonder...

• Don't ask how Sachiko could have legally adopted Yoko. You're supposed to ignore anything that doesn't make sense as you read this. It's all part of the nonsense gag humor.

⑦おさな母3

(7) CHILD MOTHER 3—

Miyuki: Oh, she has a very bad fever . . .

Yoko: (uun) Groaning.

Miyuki: We have to call a doctor.

Yoko: I'm cold Mama . . .

Yoko: Mama . . .

Yoko: (uun uun) Groaning.

Yoko: (uun uun) Groaning.

Yoko: Are you gonna kill me?

FX: (ba) *The sudden move.*

FX: (koron) *Rolling off.*

Yoko: (haa haa) *Huffing hard.*

⑧おさな母4

つづく

(8) CHILD MOTHER 4—

FX: (totete) *Rushing by.*

Sachiko: (kyaa kyaa) *Screaming.*

Text: What Yoko saw in her fading consciousness . . .

Sachiko: (kyaa kyaa kyaa) *Screaming.*

FX: (totetetete) *Rushing by.*

Sachiko: Thirty eight . . .

Sachiko: Touch . . .

Sachiko: Please heal her illness.

FX: (peko peko) *Bowing a couple of times.*

Text: . . . was the figure of Sachiko praying earnestly for Yoko's sake.

FX: (totetetetete) *Rushing by.*

Sachiko: (kyaa kyaa) *Screaming.*

Sachiko: (kyaa kyaa kyaa) *Screaming.*

FX: (totetetete) *Rushing by.*

Yoko: S—Sacchan . . .

Text below the panel: To Be Continued

Commentary:

• Regarding the title, おさな母 (osana haha), the author no longer calls Sachiko おさな妻 (osanazuma) now that the irresponsible husband is out of the picture.

• The first time the word おさな母 (osana haha) appeared in this book, I doubt if the author planned to have the Sacchan series to evolve into けものみち (kemono michi). Instead, perhaps, the idea of おさな母 (osana haha) evolved in his mind over time and crystallized in the form of けものみち (kemono michi).

Commentary:

• お百度 (ohyakudo) is a noun which represents an act of devout prayer by visiting a designated place of a temple one hundred times. 百 (hyaku) is equivalent to the number "hundred." お百度を踏む (ohyakudo o fumu) is the verb of お百度 (ohyakudo). 踏む (fumu) on its own is a verb which means "to step on."

• The reason why Sachiko is screaming as she runs back and forth is a mystery.

帰ってきた狂犬兄弟

RETURN OF MAD DOG BROTHERS

Aniki: What should we do?

Man: A—Aniki!!

Man: Now is the time for Bamboo-copter!!

Aniki: Yup!!

Aniki: So, that's what we'll do. Sorry about that, guys . . .

Aniki: Ha ha ha ha ha ha ha ha ha ha

FX: (zawa zawa) *The noise of the crowd.*

Text: — The End—

FX: (zawa zawa) *The noise of the crowd.*

中学生日記　保険体育

STUDENT'S DIARY—PHYSICAL EDUCATION

Boy: Uh?

Boy: This means . . .

Text: Physical Education

Boy: At least one girl in my class

Boy: is having a menstrual cycle right now . . .

Teacher: Argh, how boring . . .

Commentary:

• As I mentioned earlier, there's a movie called 狂犬三兄弟 (kyoken san kyodai), which translates to "Three Mad Dog Brothers." It was first released in 1972. Apparently, the 狂犬兄弟 (kyoken kyodai) part of the title of this comic strip originates from the movie.

• The author also brought back another motif from the ドラえもん (doraemon) series. It is children's manga classic in Japan, and it has been made into anime. タケコプター (take koputaa) is one of the magical tools used by ドラえもん (doraemon). タケ (take) means bamboo, and コプター (koputaa) is short for ヘリコプター (heri koputaa = helicopter). It looks like a simple 竹とんぼ (take tonbo). とんぼ (tonbo) is a dragonfly, which is why it is sometimes referred to as Bamboo Dragonfly. The magical tool was originally called ヘリトンボ (heli tonbo) before it was renamed タケコプター (take koputaa) by the creators of the classic manga. In the story, the タケコプター (take koputaa) is attached to one's head, and as soon as the switch is turned on, the person can fly around anywhere.

Commentary:

• As I mentioned earlier, there is a TV show called 中学生日記 (chugakusei nikki), which translates to "Junior High School Students' Diary." It is a dramatized reality show (or dramatized documentary film) with real students acting out scenes that depict issues they have in their lives.

• Please note, panels #1 & #2 and panels #3 & #4 are scenes taking place at different times. Panels #1 & #2 are taking place during the recess hours, while panels #3 & #4 are taking place during an English class.

• Knowing the author's sense of humor and generation, perhaps, See-Through Teacher is wearing so called sanitary panties...

しのびのもの

NINJA

FX: (suru suru) *The sound of drying her body.*

Zunmu 1: How bold Kamui is today . . .!

Zunmu 2: No, she's . . .

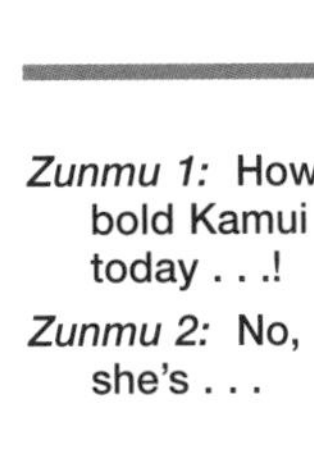

Text: Kaoru Miyu!!

FX: (kuru) *Turning.*

Zunmu: Kuwabara, kuwabara

Zunmu: Let's shit and go to bed.

DRY-MON

Girl: Arrgh.

Girl: I wish I could fly freely through the air.

Dry-mon: Leave it up to me.

FX: (paro paro) *The sound of the spinning propeller attached to the head.*

Dry-mon: I'm happy for you.

FX: (puru puru) The sound of the spinning propeller attached to the head.

Girl: . . .

Commentary:

• 由美かおる (yumi kaoru) is a Japanese actress whose career started in the 1970s. She has appeared in numerous TV shows and movies over a couple of decades. Her roles have included sexy ninja-type characters in period pieces.

• くわばら (kuwabara) is an incantation used to help avoid unpleasant and disagreeable things that befall the people who chant it.

Commentary:

• The imaginary characterドラえもん (doraemon) is once again making his appearance in this comic strip. It's obvious the author played with the name of the character here because there's a strong similarity between ドライもん (dry-mon) andドラえもん(doraemon). Also please note that the drawing of the character ドライもん (dry-mon) looks very much like the character ドラえもん (doraemon).

• Also note that ボクにまかせてよ (boku ni makaseteyo), which translates to "leave it up to me," is a typical phrase heard in the show. After all, ドラえもん(doraemon)'s mission is to help out the bespectacled boy, のび太 (nobita), with his troubles.

(9) MOTHER AND DAUGHTER

Text outside the panel: A manga series: Animal Trail

Yoko: Sacchan, you wet your bed again! You idiot!

Text: Since Sachiko adopted Yoko,

Text: it's been almost a month.

Sachiko: (kusun kusun) *Sobbing.*

Yoko: You've got to eat bell peppers too!!

Sachiko: No!!

Miyuki: Yoko-chan's getting really used to us . . .

Sachiko: No!!

Text: Miyuki was happy about it.

Commentary:

• Just laugh and enjoy the author's weird sense of humor.

• By the way, panels #3 & #4 show another example of a typical 茶の間 (chanoma). The 茶の間 (chanoma) is where the family eats its meals. It also functions as a family room.

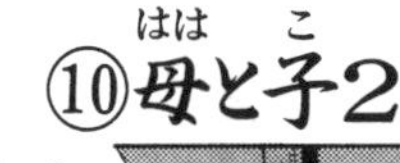

(10) MOTHER AND DAUGHTER 2

Sachiko: What should I do? I wet my bed again.

Sachiko: Yoko-tan will scold me again.

Sachiko: (een een) Crying.

Yoko: . . .

Sachiko: Oh dear, it's not wet anymore!!

Sachiko: What happened!? Was it just a dream!?

Yoko: Sacchan, you didn't wet your bed today. Very good girl.

Sachiko: Ahem!

Text: Yoko felt anxious for her stepmother.

Commentary:

• どうちまちょ (douchimacho) is どうしましょ (doushimasho), おねちょ (onecho) is おねしょ (onesho), and ちてちまった (chitechimatta) is してしまった (shiteshimatta) -- all said in baby talk. Please note that the difference between the baby talk and the proper pronunciation is "c" and "s". Apparently, Japanese pre-K kids have a hard time pronouncing "s." So the easiest way to mimic baby talk is to pronounce all "shi" and "sho" as "chi" and "cho."

• If a non-Japanese native tries speaking in Japanese with this baby talk technique, what do you think will happen? Would he/she sound adorable or irritating? Perhaps you don't want to know...

(11) BEAUTIFUL SEASON

Sachiko: (gusun gusun) *A snuffing sound, indicating that tears are welling up.*

Yoko: Sense, that's not good.

Yoko: This is how to do it!

Sachiko: (sun sun) *A light snuffing sound, indicating that she stopped crying.*

Song: Yochi, yochi.

Sensei: Heh

Text: It was good that Yoko became a happier girl.

Text: Teacher Parent Conference Room

Someone: Ha ha ha . . .

Someone: Ho ho ho . . .

Text: Sachiko thought so with great relief.

(12) CURRY RICE

Yoko: Urgh, curry again!

Sachiko: Let's eat!

Miyuki: Please bear with it, Yoko-chan.

Yoko: Humph . . .

Sachiko: . . .

Yoko: I don't want to eat curry three times a day.

Miyuki: I'm sorry. Since my bro ran off, we don't have much money.

つづく

Sachiko: I'd better do something about it . . .

Text: As a mother, Sachiko is resolved to get a job.

Text below the panel: ***To Be Continued***

Commentary:

• センセ (sense) is short for 先生 (sensei). As I mentioned earlier, 先生 (sensei) is a commonly used term for respectfully addressing someone. Usually it's used to address people like teachers, professors, lawyers, doctors and politicians.

• へえー (heh) is a type of exclamation indicating that someone is impressed by understanding or perceiving something.

Commentary:

• Believe it or not, カレーライス (karee raisu = curry rice) is one of the staple dishes eaten in Japanese households. The Japanese curry originates from India, but Indian curry did not come directly to Japan; instead, it was first brought to England—after all, India was British colony. The British invented "curry power" in the 19th century and used wheat flour to thicken the curry. During the Meiji Era, when Japan was very open to Western culture, the Japanese imported this curry from England. During WW II, curry rice was eaten by every soldier, and as a result, it rapidly spread all around Japan.

• Although there are some variations, curry cooked in Japanese households almost always has some onions, carrots and potatoes. Usually chicken, pork or beef is added to its ingredients. Unlike Indian curry, individual spices are not added to the mix, but instead, ready made curry paste is used to flavor the dish.

血の叫び

BLOOD'S SCREAM

私ユーコ15歳でェす

顔はうつさないでネ

Yuko: I'm Yuko, a fifteen-year-old.

Yuko: Please don't show my face.

Yuko: Oh no, it's embarrassing!

Yuko: Oh no!

なにが"ユーコのH体験"じゃ〜〜〜!!
作ったやつ出てこんか〜〜〜い!!

Man 1: What the heck is this "Yuko's Experience"!?

Man 2: C'mon, who produced this video!?

Commentary:

• There are two things going on. First of all, if the girl is telling the truth, this is child pornography, which is illegal. Second, due to government censorship, adult videos in Japan are forbidden from showing male and female genitalia.

• The point here is that with her face and pretty much all of her naked body are blurred, this so-called fifteen-year-old could easily be a middle-aged woman. And not only that, what's the point of an adult video if you can't see anything?

シリーズ
かわしまにっき
川島日記

このごろ
ウジゴロシ
みないねェ

ウジゴロシ

Series
Kawashima's Diary

Right: I don't see Maggot Killers around of late.

Text on the label of the bottle: Maggot Killers

Commentary:

• This must be another way of saying that there are more modern toilets in Japan than old-style ones. The bottles of ウジゴロシ (ujigoroshi = maggot killers) must have been used when people didn't have flush toilets available. You see, the flies like to lay eggs on the excrement, so people needed maggot killers to keep the eggs from hatching.

絞死刑 (こうしけい)

DEATH PENALTY BY HANGING

Sazae-san: Please watch us again next week.

FX: (ngagugu) *a sound of Sazae-san choking to death*

Text: Saze e-san produced by Nagisa Oshima—The End

RUN AWAY SEASON

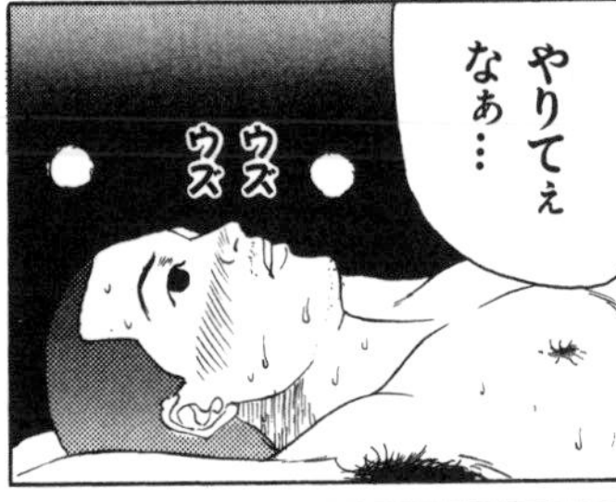

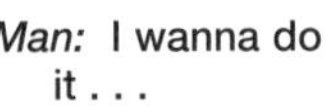

Man: I wanna do it . . .

FX: (uzu uzu) *having an urge*

Woman: No way.

いやよ いやよ♡
いいべ!? いいべ!?

Woman: No, I don't!

Man: Why not!? Can't we!?

Woman: No way. I don't wanna.

FX: (su su su su) *Swift and quick move.*

Man: Why not!? Can't we!?

Text: ***The End***

Commentary:

• An award winning movie director, 大島渚 (oshima nagisa), began his career in the late 1950s. He has made numerous movies and documentary films, and he also appeared on various TV shows as a guest personality.

• The character that appears on panel #2 is similar to the anime character サザエさん (Sazae-san). As I mentioned earlier, the comic strip version of サザエさん (Sazae-san) started in 1949. The anime version began in 1969, and it's still on-air.

• The gag is how the author illustrates 大島渚 (oshima nagisa)'s style of filmmaking by bringing サザエさん (Sazae-san) into the picture. Take note that the image of サザエさん (Sazae-san) is an ordinary housewife with a happy-go-lucky personality.

Commentary:

• You choose whether to laugh or vomit.

• And, I'll leave it up to your imagination what the man wants to do, and how...

それぞれの夏 SUMMER FOR EACH

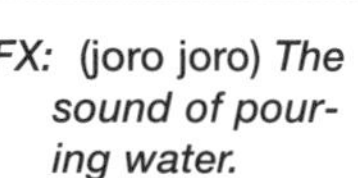

FX: (joro joro) *The sound of pouring water.*

FX: (jii) *Staring hard.*

Man 1: This "Urinating Girl" is so real . . .

FX: (joro joro) *The sound of pouring water.*

Man 2: She makes my heart beat faster . . .

Commentary:

• So, the Three Musketeers are aging. Look at their balding heads.

• And, the dirty old men are getting excited by a fountain...

由美かおる忍法帖 KAORU YUMI NINPOUCHO

Shinobi: Please tell me one thing before I die . . .

Shinobi: For Heaven's sake, how old are you?

Text: The dying shinobi could no longer hear the words she whispered.

Text below the panel: ***The End***

Commentary:

• 忍法帖 (ninpoucho) is a word that almost always appears in the Ninja novels of 1960s written by Huutarou Yamada, a renowned novelist of popular entertainment. Yamada called the professional assassins 忍者 (ninja) and art of しのび (忍, shinobi) 忍法 (ninpou). The terms he created went on to become the standard usage.

• As I mentioned earlier, 由美かおる (yumi kaoru) is a Japanese actress whose career started in 1970s. She has appeared in numerous TV shows and movies over a couple of decades. Her roles included the sexy ninja-type characters in period pieces. Now you know what makes this comic strip funny to many Japanese readers who watched her over years.

(13) WORKING MOM

Text outside the panel: A manga series: ***Animal Trail***

Text: Sachiko took on a job.

Sachiko: You can't cross the street yet.

Sachiko: You must wait until it turns green.

Girl 1: Isn't that new Green Obasan cute?

Girl 2: Yup. She's so cute!

Miyuki: Green Obasan doesn't get paid, you know . . .

FX: (gaan) An expression indicating that she's shocked and feels as if a rock has been dropped on her head.

Commentary:

• みどりのおばさん (midori no obasan) is someone who helps children (who are commuting to school) cross a busy street safely. みどり (midori) means green, and おばさん, in this instance, means woman. みどりのおばさん (midori no obasan) was first introduced in 1959 in the Tokyo area, and it quickly spread around the country. At the time, the purpose for creating this job was both to help support unemployed single mothers and to help reduce traffic accidents involving children.

• For decades, large numbers of みどりのおばさん (midori no obasan) could be seen on street corners near schools all across Japan. However, since the mid 80s, the みどりのおばさん (midori no obasan) have declined in numbers. The budget cuts are a big reason for this. Some communities nowadays have volunteer みどりのおばさん (midori no obasan) instead of paid ones.

⑭働く母2

(14) WORKING MOM 2—

Sachiko: Kurin, kurin, kurin.

Sachiko: Kurin, kurin, kurin.

Sachiko: Are you going out?

Old Man: Ho ho ho

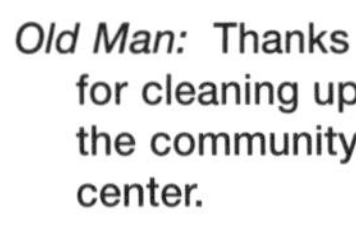

Old Man: Thanks for cleaning up the community center.

Old Man: Here's a candy for your trouble.

FX: (gaan) *An expression indicating that she's shocked and feels as if a rock has been dropped on her head.*

Commentary:

• Sachiko's saga continues, as she searches for a paying job...

⑮働く母3

(15) WORKING MOM 3

FX: (miin miin) *The sound made by cicadas.*

Sachiko: (kusun kusun) Sobbing.

Man: We'll buy all these tofu . . .

FX: (miin miin) *The sound made by cicadas.*

Sachiko: (gusu gusu) *A snuffing sound due to sobbing.*

Woman: So, don't cry anymore, Sacchan . . .

Commentary:

• From the look of it, Sachiko finally got a job selling tofu, except that she fell and spoiled them all... It's tough to be a single mom, huh?

⑯働く母4

(16) WORKING MOM 4

Boy 1: Hey, wait up, Yoko!

Boy 2: Stupid, you!

こいつのパンツ穴あいてやがんだぜ
おめン家ビンボだろバーカァ

Boy 1: Her panties have holes you know.

Boy 2: You're from a poor family, aren't you, idiot?

はーただいま〜〜〜
なんだろ
よおこちゃんへ

Yoko: Haah, I'm home!!

Yoko: What's this?

Text: For Yoko-chan

…さっちゃん…
給料がでた佐智子だった―
あたらしいぱんつです
さちこ

つづく

Text: New panties for you.—*Sachiko*

Yoko: . . . Sacchan . . .

Text: Sachiko finally received a paycheck—

*Text below the panel: **To Be Continued***

Commentary:

• おめン家 (omenchi) is a colloquial way of saying おまえの家 (omaenouchi), which translates to "your family"—in this instance.

• はー (haah) is a deep sigh.

• ただいま (tadaima) is the short form of ただいま帰りました (tadaima kaerimashita), which translates to "I have just returned home." It's customary for people in Japan to say this to announce their arrival home.

バブル2世

BUBBLE THE SECOND

砂の嵐に
かくされた
バブルの塔に
住んでいる

Text: He lives in the Tower of Bubble, hidden inside the sandstorm.

Text: He is the super human boy,

Text: Bubble the Second!!

Boy: Rodem!!

Rodem: Yes, sir.

Boy: Transform into a girl!!

Rodem: Not again, Boss . . .

Commentary:

• This comic strip is a parody of the well-known anime called バビル二世 (babiru nisei), which is known as "Babel II" in America. The manga artist 横浜光輝 (yokohama mitsuteru) first conceived of the title in manga format, and it was eventually made into anime. バビル二世 (babiru nisei) lives in the Tower of Babel, which is hidden inside the sandstorm, and has guardian servants, one of which is the black panther, who can transform himself.

• 横浜光輝 (yokohama mitsuteru)'s most famous manga is Tetsujin #28 Go. It was made into an anime and eventually released in America under the title Gigantor in 1960s. 横浜光輝 (yokohama mitsuteru) is unarguably one of the most prolific, imaginative and creative manga artists in Japan. He has had a profound influenced on Japanese anime. He passed away in April 2004.

シリーズ
川島日記

1992

職場から逃げられないよう片眉剃ったー

ル〜ラララ〜

Series Kawashima's Diary

1992—I shaved one of my eyebrows so that I won't be tempted to get away from my work—

Singing: Lu Lalalaaa

Commentary:

• The author must've thought that the embarrassing look on his face was enough to keep him at work.

• If you feel like it, you might want to dream up other ways of keeping yourself at work. But really, most Americans aren't like Japanese when it comes to feeling obliged to work long hours—right?

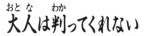

大人は判ってくれない

GROWNUPS DON'T UNDERSTAND

Text: ♥I am a flight attendant. ♥I just started doing an "H-type" part time job♥. Will you buy that uncensored photo for two thousand yen? Send it to OO Post Office, Tokyo 100, Attn: Akemi

FX: (doki doki doki) Throbbing hearts.

Text: ♥I am a seventeen-year-old "H-type", female high school student. ♥It's embarrassing, but I'll let you have my OO photo for two thousand yen ♥ Send it to OO Post Office, Tokyo 100, Attn: Sayaka

FX: (doki doki doki) Throbbing hearts.

Commentary:

• An "H-type" job is, of course, that "ecchi" type work, i.e., something to do with sex or lust. Due to government censorship, Japanese media is forbidden from showing male and female genitalia, and therefore, many young people in Japan have little opportunity to get their hands on uncensored material.

• In this comic strip, the author is making fun of the youth who end up paying for bogus photos.

明日 (あした) — TOMORROW

Man: Oh.

Man: The Arachnid-woman's up there . . .

Man: She's wearing pink today . . .

Man: That means . . .

Man: It'll be black tomorrow!!

Commentary:

• When there's an obsession over woman's panties, even superheroes aren't safe as the author changes the character to Arachnidwoman— and of course, she must wear a lovely outfit with her underwear showing.

転身の頌 (てんしん しょう) — PANEGYRIC TRANSFORMATION

Panty: One day, when I woke up,

Panty: I found myself as a panty.

Panty: This is See-Through Teacher's!!

Panty: Great!! Lucky me!!

FX: (kotsu kotsu) *The sound of light footsteps made by heeled shoes.*

Panty: It's embarrassing . . .

Commentary:

• One morning, a boy finds himself turned into the panties of スケスケ先生 (sukesuke sensei = See-Through Teacher). He thinks he's lucky, until he realizes what it feels like to be stared at by everyone.

• The intimate (and perhaps private) image he had of his being her panties proved to be totally wrong. There's no such a thing as privacy as far as See-Through Teacher's panties are concerned.

⑰健さんの心

KEN-SAN'S HEART

連載マンガ けものみち

Text outside the panel: A manga series: Animal Trail

Sachiko: S—Sir . . .

Sachiko: Here's the fried potatoes you ordered . . .

FX: (karon) *The slight sound made by the very last fried potatoes.*

Ken-san: You're . . . hungry, aren't you . . .?

FX: (kokun) *Nod*

Ken-san: Have another piece then . . .

Sachiko: Ahn.

Commentary:

• 健さん (ken-san) in this comic strip is supposed to be the actor, 高倉健 (takakura ken). He is a well known actor who first debuted in the 1950s. He went on to launch an international career in films like Black Rain and Mr. Baseball (1990). Over the years, he appeared in more than 200 films.

• 高倉健 (takakura ken) has a persona that embodies both 義理 (giri) and 人情 (ninjo). This carries the image of something that is not sweet in nature, but rather reserved and somberly austere. 義理 (giri) is a sense of justice, duty, obligation and honor. 人情 (ninjo) is the emotion which makes us human. His sense of 人情 (ninjo) is deeply felt, but not openly displayed.

• The sweet, fatherly action on the part of 健さん (ken-san) in panels #3 & #4 is likely to appear humorous to many Japanese readers.

⑱母は告白する

(18) MOTHER CONFESSES

Sachiko: What shall I do? I'm fired again . . .

Sachiko: Miyuki-tan will be upset . . .

Miyuki: Welcome home.

FX: (pachi pachi pachi) *Clapping hands.*

Yoko: Wow

Miyuki: Happy birthday, Oneh-san. You're three years old now!

Text: Sachiko could not bring herself to tell them.

⑲母は告白する2

(19) MOTHER CONFESSES 2—

Sachiko: You know, Miyuki-tan, I got—

Miyuki: Here, Oneh-san, a piece of cake for you! Open your mouth wide.

Sachiko: (kyaah!) Girlish scream of delight.

Sachiko: Yoko-tan, today, Mommy got—

つづく

Yoko: Here, a present for you. A new jar of honey!

Text: Honey

Sachiko: (kyaah!) *Girlish scream of delight.*

Text: Sachiko is troubled.

Text below the panel: ***To Be Continued***

Commentary:

• クビになる (kubi ni naru), when literally translated, means "I've become a neck." Imagine someone without a body—a gruesome vision—a dead man. The man is dead—the man is terminated. In other words, when someone becomes a neck, it means that person is terminated (i.e. being fired from work)! Now, the Japanese words, クビになる (kubi ni naru), make sense, doesn't it?

Commentary:

• Cake was first introduced to Japan by the Portuguese in the 16th century. But it wasn't until the early 20th century that it became commercially available. At first, it was considered a luxury item, and only the wealthy could enjoy it. It took half a century before the general population began appreciating cake. Even then, it was considered a pricey, special treat, and most of the people bought it only on special occasions.

• Nowadays, celebrating one's birthday with a birthday cake has become common in Japan. This modern custom appears to be rooted in Japanese tradition combined with commercialism. Traditionally, sweetened お餅 (omochi = pounded rice) with sugared red bean paste was offered at special occasions, like weddings and memorial services. This custom made the idea of a birthday cake seem natural, and when it was coupled with an appetite for all things Western, the idea of birthday cakes took off.

シリーズ
かわしまにっき
川島日記

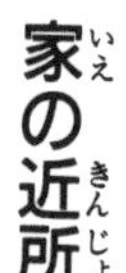

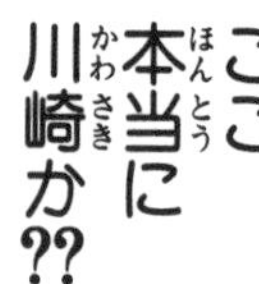

Series **Kawashima's Diary**

Text: My neighborhood.
Is this really Kawasaki??

Text: Watch out for raccoons.

Commentary:

• Before the World War, 川崎 (Kawasaki) area was a rural community, boasting of its agricultural and marine produce. However, just before WWII, heavy industry developed rapidly and pollution became a major problem. For quite some time, 川崎 (Kawasaki) has been viewed as a polluted, industrialized area, which is incompatible with wildlife.

EPITOME

Text: Departing from Shinjuku—

Text: The first train that departs on the Odakyu Line—

FX: (goton goton) The rattling sound of the moving train.

FX: (gototon goto-ton) The rattling sound of the moving train.

Text: Scary—

FX: (paan) *The sound of the train rushing by.*

Commentary:

• The biggest gay town in Japan is 二丁目 (Nichome) in the 新宿 (Shinjuku) area.

• 始発電車 (shihatsu densha) is the very first train that operates in the morning. A typical person that uses 始発電車 (shihatsu densha) is someone who stayed up late the night before and missed the last train.

• This comic strip is making a joke by showing how the 始発電車 (shihatsu densha) that departs from 新宿 (Shinjuku) is loaded with transvestites. Who else would stay up late in that part of town?

Nichome

泣き上戸

NAKI JOGO

Quote: Tink!

Quote: Gokyu gokyu gokyu . . .

Quote: Puhaah!!

Aniki: You sure that urine therapy works?

Man: How do I know, Aniki?

Commentary:

• I've got to admit that I thought the author made up 尿療法 (nyo-ryoho = urine therapy). But when I did some research, I discovered that it's real. I don't know about you, but to me the idea of gulping down one's own urine like a glass of orange juice is a little nauseating. But apparently there are millions of people around the world who believe in this therapy, and they drink their own urine on a daily basis. And believe it or not, this practice has been around for centuries.

• I find it hard to imagine, but they claim that fresh urine is sterile and devoid of any pathogens—unless a person has a urinary tract or kidney infection. Also, they believe it contains helpful nutrients! Supposedly, bacteria grow quickly in urine after it exits the body, so a person can't just leave it in a cup for later—it has to be consumed right away. Anyhow, enough said. Believe what you want.

けんかえれじい

ELEGY OF BLOWS

Girl: Whoa!

FX: (fuwa) *Blown away.*

Girl: Thank you so much.

Boy: Ha ha ha

Boy: Er—Will you . . . go out with me . . . for some tea . . .?

Boy: Daaah!!!

Commentary:

• けんか (kenka) means "to quarrel or fight." えれじい (eregii) is the English word "elegy."

• だあー (daaah) is a forceful Kiai-like yell of concentration.

• The old man lost his hat, just like the girl did, but in his attempt to find it, he upsets the boy. In a raging temper, the boy attacks the innocent old man.

• This is an elegy for anyone who happens to be at the wrong place at a wrong time...

男の世界ダー第2章ー

IT'S THE MAN'S WORLD—PART 2 —

Fat boy: Let's go, new kid.

FX: (yurari) *A wavering sort of move.*

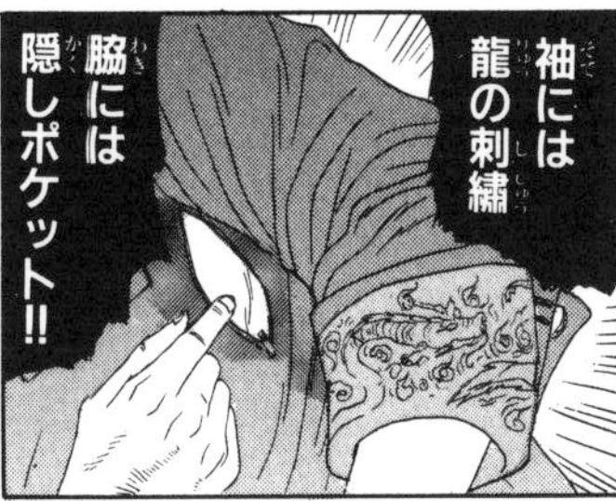

Fat boy: My sleeves are embroidered with dragons.

Fat boy: Under my arm is a hidden pocket!!

Fat boy: The inner linings are embroidered with tigers.

FX: (don) *A dramatic presentation.*

Fat boy: And, it's the high waist pants!!

Fat boy: If you got that, stop acting haughty.

FX: (nura nura) *A slippery and wavering sort of move.*

Commentary:

• Yes, it's that big faced boy who thinks the world of himself. He believes that what he wears represents who he is (i.e. the cool ruler of all boys at school), and therefore, everyone should bow down to him. You can either see yourself in him, sympathize with him, laugh at him, or pity him.

サナギマン

SANAGIMAN

Chrysalis Man: Ah . . .

Chrysalis Man: What a nice day!

Chrysalis Man: Indeed!!

FX: (dochu) *A firm step, pressing down upon a squishy substance.*

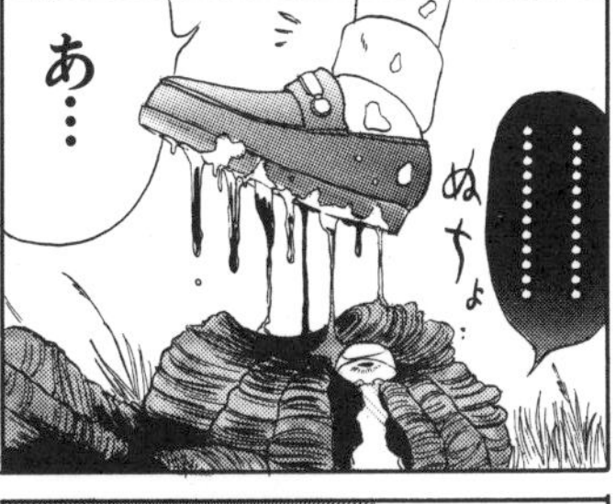

Chrysalis Man: . . .

FX: (nucho) *Pulling out a squishy substance.*

Girl: Argh . . .

Girl: Can't believe I stepped in someone's turd first thing in the morning!!

Girl: Oh no!

Commentary:

• サナギ (蛹, sanagi) means chrysalis. In the 1970s, the manga versions (as well as the TV anime versions) of サナギマン (sanagi man) were released. As the title suggests, サナギマン (sanagi man) is a weak chrysalis of a superhero called イナズマン (inazu man). Later on, the title サナギマン (sanagi man) was changed to イナズマン (inazu man). It was mainly because the weak and not-so-sharp looking サナギマン (sanagi man) was less palatable to the audience than the cool character イナズマン (inazu man).

• In this series, a boy transforms into サナギマン (sanagi man) first, before he turns into the powerful イナズマン (inazu man). Just as with any traditional superheroes, イナズマン (inazu man) fights evil and brings about justice.

• Given the history of this superhero, many Japanese readers will view this comic with a sense of nostalgia.

⑳おさなママ

連載マンガ けものみち

(20) CHILD MOTHER

Text outside the panel: A manga series: Animal Trail

Text: Mama wanted!! Bar . . .

Man: Why did you choose this job?

Sachiko: Ahem.

Sachiko: It's because I am a Mama.

Text: Thus . . .

Text: Sachiko got a job as a Mama at a bar.

Commentary:

• As I mentioned earlier, a female manager of a bar in Japan is usually called ママ (mama).

• Don't ask me how Sachiko could get this job, but it's funny in its own absurdist way.

㉑おさなママ2

(21) CHILD MOTHER 2—

FX: (kokkuri kokkuri) *Her head is nodding, indicating that she is falling asleep.*

Sachiko: Miyuki-tan . . .

FX: (ngaga) *Making noise in her sleep.*

FX: (kokkuri kokkuri) *Her head is nodding, indicating that she is falling asleep.*

Sachiko: Miyuki-tan?

Sachiko: She finally fell asleep . . .

FX: (suru suru) *Slowly and quietly pull over.*

FX: (suu suu) *The steady, rhythmic sound of sleep—sound asleep.*

つづく

Man: Mama, you're late!

Text: Sachiko juggles between her home life and her job.

Sachiko: Hmm

Text below the panel: To Be Continued

Commentary:

• おねむ (onemu) comes from お眠り (onemuri), which means "to fall asleep." Usually, one uses the word おねむ (onemu) to refer to the sleeping state of a baby.

シリーズ
川島日記

Series Kawashima's Diary

ココロに
沁みるぜ
梶芽衣子の
「怨み節」

Text: Meiko Kaji's "Uramibushi" touches my heart deeply.
Song: Urami . . . bu . . .shi . . .

Commentary:

• 梶芽衣子 (kaji meiko) sang the theme song called 怨み節 (urami bushi) for the movie series 女囚さそり (joshuu sasori = female prisoner, Sasori). The movie was first released in the early 70s. 梶芽衣子 (kaji meiko) acted the role of さそり (sasori) in the movie too.

• 怨み (urami) means grudge or hatred, and 節 (fushi), in this instance, means melody or rhythm. 女囚さそり (joshuu sasori) is a frightening thriller, with さそり (sasori) portrayed as a violent fugitive, whose fierceness is beyond imagination.

Joshuu Sasori

まほうつかい

WITCH

Old man: Hi!! How's it going?

FX: (shuta) *The swift motion.*

Woman: Oh, it's you, Masakittsuan.

Woman: He's incredibly energetic.

FX: (do do do do do do) *A loud sound reminiscent of a stampede.*

Woman: He doesn't look 89 years old.

Girl: Humph.

Girl: Here.

Girl: No one will notice that the gramps is already dead . . .

Father: Don't fool around like that!

Girl: I'm sorry, Dad!!

Commentary:

• And what girl would like to pretend to be her grandfather, I wonder? Maybe, for her, the fun lies in tricking the others.

• Of course, this is the author's version of how a witch would use her magic...

蒼ざめた日曜日

PALE SUNDAY

Zunmu 1: Yep, yep, there's our tormentress Kamui . . .

Zunmu 2: Nope . . . that one is—

Text: Ruriko P. Asa!!

Zunmu: Kuwabara, kuwabara!!

Zunmu: Let's shit and go to bed.

Commentary:

• People chant the くわばら (kuwabara), a special incantation, to help avoid unpleasant and disagreeable things that might befall them.

• It is obvious that the author is making fun of an actress called 浅丘ルリ子 (asaoka ruriko). Born in July 1940, she launched her career in the mid 1950s. Somehow, her slim frame and her love life (the latest affair being with a man 19 years younger than she is) reminds me a bit of Cher.

SAIKAKU ICHIDAI ONNA

Woman: Ah, it's not permissible.

Man 1: It's alright, isn't it . . .?

FX: (kuru kuru) *Spinning around.*

Woman: Ah!

Woman: Oh no!

Man 2: Don't copy the Western style!

夕やけ雲

SUNSET CLOUDS

Teacher: What's wrong, Yamagishi-kun?

Yamagishi: I'd like to ask you a question.

Yamagishi: See-Through Teacher, why aren't . . .

Yamagishi: your panties see-through?

Text: ***— To Be Continued***

Commentary:

• 西鶴 (saikaku) is a classic Japanese poet and novelist known as 井原西鶴 (ihara saikaku), one of the most influential literary figures of 17th-century Japanese literature. He wrote many racy tales of the love and monetary affairs of the merchant class and the demimonde. One of his fictional stories, 好色一代女 (koshoku ichidai onna), which means "The Life of an Amorous Woman," is about how the heroine constantly gets in trouble because of her own lustful nature. Apparently, the movie called 西鶴一代女 (saikaku ichidai onna), which was made in the 1950s, was based on this novel.

• So, about the gag—in a Japanese period piece like this, it's quite unusual to show full-frontal nudity. Usually a scene like the one shown in panel #3 would take place behind a sliding door or some other form of screen, leaving the viewers to their imaginations. Hence, the censored shot, with the vase placed strategically to obstruct her full nudity, is apparently not acceptable to this imaginary film director.

Commentary:

• Due to government censorship, Japanese media is forbidden from showing male or female genitalia. And of course, the rule applies to manga as well.

• However, in this comic strip, the boy can't help but ask the obvious question. This is both a self-reflexive joke and a statement on Japanese society and censorship.

㉒如何なる星の下に

(22) NO MATTER UNDER WHAT STAR

いいえ あたっちー わ♬
ちゃちょりぢゃ のおんなっ♬

Text outside the panel: A manga series: Animal Trail

Sachiko: Nope. I am a . . .

Sachiko: woh-man of ja Schu-corpio.

おきの ちゅむまでっ
わらうが いーわっ♬

Sachiko: Until you're sha-tis-fied,

Sachiko: go on and laugh.

Someone: Please give our Mama, Sachiko-san, a big hand!!

FX: (pachi pachi pachi pachi . . .) *Clapping hands*

Text: Sachiko has expanded her fan base by singing live.

㉓如何なる星の下に2

(23) NO MATTER UNDER WHAT STAR 2—

Girl 1: That new kid is saucy.

Girl 2: Let's torture her, shall we . . .?

Sachiko: Huh? My thing's missing!!

Sachiko: What shall I do?

Sachiko: A mound of poo on my shoe!!

Sachiko: Why? How come?

Master: Don't be cruel to her!

Text: Master cares about Mama.

Text below the panel: ***To Be Continued***

Commentary:

• サチコ (sachiko) is singing a well-known song called さそり座の女 (sasoriza no onna), which translates to read "Woman of Scorpio." サチコ (sachiko)'s vocal abilities are not quite developed, which is obvious from the way she miss-pronounces words.

• さそり座の女 (sasoriza no onna) was first sung by 美川憲一 (mikawa kenichi) in 1973, and it became a big hit. It is still adored by many Japanese, and it's often sung at Karaoke bars.

Commentary:

• ヤキ (焼き, yaki) means "to broil or burn." 入れる (ireru) means "to put or insert."

• ヤキ入れ (yaki ireru) is a term that refers to a "heat treatment process." When used in sword making, it is about hardening the steel by heating, then quenching the blade. However, as slang, what ヤキ入れ (yaki ireru) really means is to torture or torment someone by bullying them or playing cruel tricks on them. What the girls did in this comic strip is a classic form of ヤキ入れ (yaki ireru).

山の呼び声

CALLING VOICES OF THE MOUN-TAINS

FX: (kyoro kyoro) *Looking around.*

Old man 1: Oh!

Old man 1: There it is . . .

Old man 2: You've got good eyes!

Old man 1: Erohons are the best for mountain hiking.

Old man 2: Yep, that's my favorite part of hiking in the mountains.

Commentary:

• エロ本 (erohon)'s エロ (ero) is short for the English word "erotic" and 本 (hon) means "book." エロ本 (erohon) means a magazine that generally appeals to the carnal desires of the male population, like "Playboy" or "Hustler."

• The Three Musketeers have returned—this time as old men with fully bald heads. Somehow, their unceasing desire to seek out sexual excitement can find comfort in a mountain hike—however, it is questionable if, in real life, one could find エロ本 (erohon) along the trails of Japanese mountains...

シリーズ
かわしまにっき
川島日記

Series **Kawashima's Diary**

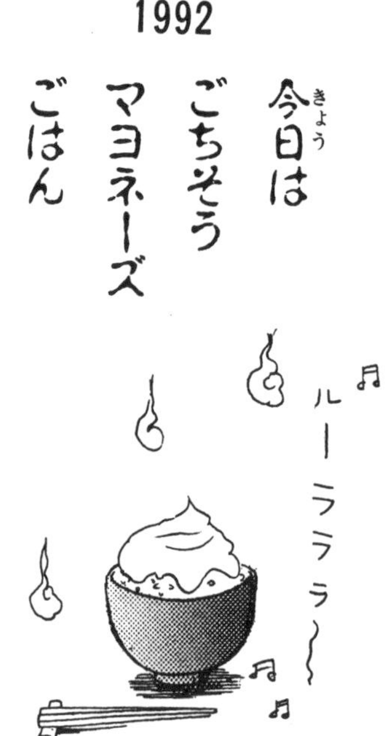

1992
今日は
ごちそう
マヨネーズ
ごはん
ルーララ～

※刑務所ではない

1992

Text: Today's treat is rice with mayonaise.

Song: Lu lalala

Note: This isn't at a prison.

Commentary:

• マヨネーズ (mayonezu = mayonnaise) was first introduced to Japan in 1925 by a Japanese company called Q.P. Corporation. Since 1958, the soft squeeze bottle of Q.P. Mayonnaise has become one of the items found in most Japanese households.

• It's just that, I can't imagine rice with mayonnaise being considered a treat. Imagine having a slice of white bread with a generous potion of mayonnaise—would you consider that a treat? We have to wonder if the author, as a fishmonger, was paid minimum wage...

男の世界ダ—第3章—

IT'S A MAN'S WORLD—PART 3 —

Fat boy: I heard you took care of my bro.

Boy: So what?

Fat boy: Humph, Kankoh straight, huh?

Fat boy: So not cool.

Fat boy: Dirty Marie Banana Pants!!

FX: (baan) *A dramatic presentation.*

Fat boy: If you got that, stop acting so stuck up.

FX: (nura nura) *A slippery and wavering sort of move.*

Commentary:

• 世話 (sewa) means "take care" or "look after." When the fat boy said that the other boy took care of his brother, he meant his brother was beaten up by the other boy.

• カンコー (kankoh) is a brand of school uniform. ダーティ マリー バナナ パンツ (daatii marii banana pantsu = Dirty Marie Banana Pants) is another brand of super-baggy pants, made as a variation of school uniform.

ずん子と螢の歌

THE BALLAD OF ZUNKO AND A FIREFLY

Sensei: Zunko, look at the firefly . . .

Zunko: Oh yeah.

Zunko: Oh, no, Shienshie's being bold.

Zunko: What shall I do?

Zunko: No way, on a day like this,

Zunko: I'm wearing mega undies that go all the way up to my navel.

Zunko: No way.

Zunko: It's so embarrassing!!

Commentary:

• あんれま (anrema) is あらまぁ (aramaa), しぇんしぇ (shienshie) is 先生 (sensei), やんだ (yanda) is いやだ (iyada), どうすっぺ (dohsuppe) is どうしよう (dohshiyou), and はんずかす (hanzukasu) is はずかしい (hazukashii) with a heavy accent. オラ (ora) is わたし (watashi) in a rural dialect.

• This reminds me of the 2001 movie called *Bridget Jones's Diary*, if you know what I mean... Many Japanese girls must share a similar sentiment—but really, she didn't need to punch him so hard.

㉔人間の絆
連載マンガ けものみち
きゃ
きゃ
あたちね ママに なったの
きゃーっ

(24) HUMAN BONDS

Text outside the panel: A manga series: ***Animal Trail***

Sachiko: (kya kya) *Delightful noise made by a happy girl at play.*

Sachiko: I became a Mama.

Sachiko: (kyaaah) *The girlish shriek of delight.*

Sachiko: That's why I'm so busy.

FX: (sesse) *Working diligently.*

おもいきって 告白したのに
かわいー！
わかって もらえない 佐智子だった—

Text: Despite her bold confession . . .

Miyuki: So cute!

Text: No one understands Sachiko.

Commentary:

- And, you know why.

㉕人間の絆2

(25) HUMAN BONDS 2—

Sachiko: (kya kya) Delightful noise made by a happy girl at play.

Man: Yoh, Mama, long time no see!

Sachiko: Kyaah♥

Woman: Mama, hurry and come to the bar. I'll be waiting for you.

Miyuki: . . .

Text: Sachiko would rather Miyuki didn't see the adult world.

Sachiko: . . .

Commentary:

• The man in panel #2 is a customer at the bar where Sachiko works.

• The woman in panel #3 is one of the employees at the bar where Sachiko works. Apparently, the woman no longer despises Sachiko...

㉖人間の絆3

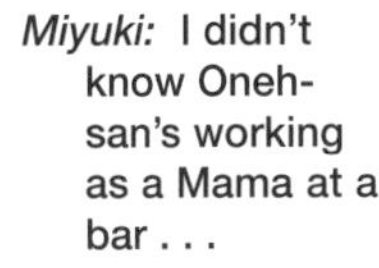

(26) HUMAN BONDS 3—

Miyuki: I didn't know Oneh-san's working as a Mama at a bar . . .

FX: (suu suu) *The steady, rhythmic sound of sleep—sound asleep.*

Miyuki: Oneh-san.

FX: (gyu . . .) *Hold tight.*

Miyuki: We've allowed you to suffer so much hardship . . .

Miyuki: Compared with the first time I met you . . .

Miyuki: You've gotten a lot smaller!!

Text: Miyuki is resolved to help Sachiko at the bar.

Text below the panel: ***To Be Continued***

つづく

Commentary:

• And, it's true, Sachiko looks a lot smaller (and younger) than the first time they met. You may recall that they first met at Sachiko's wedding.

もう明日はこない

THERE'S NO TOMORROW ANYMORE

Man: Arachnid-woman's there . . .

Text: Goodbye.

Man: What!?

Man: H—Hey, you!!

FX: (sususu) *Swiftly and quietly.*

Man: Please wait!

Text: I heard no one ever saw her again.

Text: ***— The End—***

Commentary:

• So, Arachnidwoman knew how to convey her message—i.e., she knew men always looked up at her panties.

渚のテンプラロック

TEMPURA ROCK ON THE BEACH

FX: (puri puri puri puri) *Sexy hip swing.*

FX: (zee zee zee zee zee) *Breathing hard.*

FX: (haa haa) *Huffing hard.*

Man: We've done the Monroe Walk Full Marathon, Sensei!!

Sensei: See, you can do it if you try!!

Commentary:

• テンプラ (tenpura = tempura) is a dish that was originally brought to Japan by the Potuguese in the 16th century. Gradually it changed its form, and by the 19th century, it became a vital part of Japanese cuisine. Various fresh seafood and vegetables are deep fried in tempura batter and served while they're still hot. Tempura dip and a small mound of grated radish are served along with it.

• As I mentioned earlier, "Monroe Walk" has become a term in Japan that means a sexy style of walking similar to what Marilyn Monroe did—swinging her hips.

• So the boys are rock 'n rolling all day long on the beach, frying themselves like pieces of tempura. It's another example of the distinct author's sense of humor...

あいもかわらず

JUST AS EVER

Text: Re-imported Version

We sell adult videos

1 video . . . 5,000 Yen

3 videos . . . 9,000 Yen

10 videos . . . 25,000 Yen

1xx Tokyo, xx District

FX: (doki doki doki doki) *Throbbing heart.*

FX: (fuu) *Blowing smoke.*

FX: (pui) *Look away—not friendly at all.*

Commentary:

• 裏 (ura) means the reverse side, back or opposite. 裏ビデオ (ura bideo) means uncensored (and mostly illegal) adult video.

• This is another elegy showing a deprived youth in search of uncensored adult videos... Those boys never give up, do they?

FATHER'S STUDY

FX: (basa) *The sound of the magazine falling down.*

Boy: Oops.

Boy: Th—

Boy: This is—

Boy: the See-Through Teacher!!

Text: High School Girl

See-Through Love

Text: ***To Be Continued—***

Commentary:

• Apparently, before the See-Through Teacher became a school teacher, she was a media sensation as the girl of See-Through Love.

• The saga of the boy and the See-Through Teacher continues. Who can guess what's coming next?

シリーズ
かわしまにっき
川島日記

魂(ソウル)に
沁(し)みるぜ
「不良番長(ふりょうばんちょう)」の
テーマ

ラリパ
ラリパッパ
ラリパッパ

Series Kawashima's Diary

Text: Theme song from *"Furyo Bancho"* touches my soul.

FX: Lari pap lari pappa lari pappa

Commentary:

• 不良番長 (furyo bancho) is a series of 16 movies made in late 60s through early 70s, first of which was released in 1968. 不良 (furyo) is a general term that refers to juvenile delinquents. 番長 (bancho) means "boss." The 不良番長 (furyo bancho) are a series of action films, with silly and predictable plots and loads of gags. Apparently, "lari lari pappa" is a recognizable phrase in the theme song for this series.

もしかして中年

I MIGHT BE MIDDLE-AGED

Man: X day of O month, a woman has . . .

Man: fallen asleep against my back.

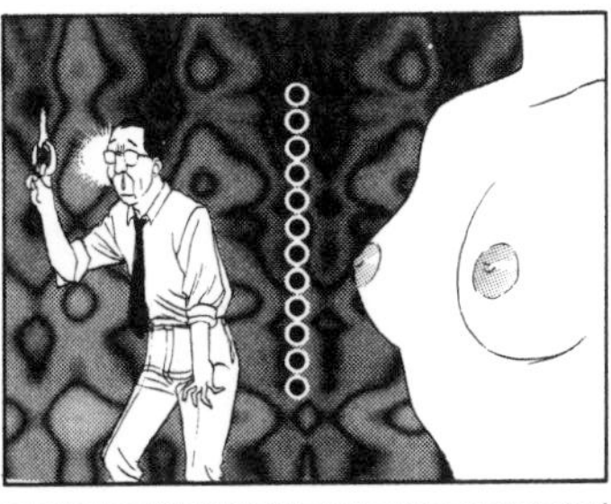

Man: I didn't know what to do, but . . .

Man: For the time being, I tried grinding—

FX: (pii pipii) *The whistling sound.*

FX: (myuin myuin) *Moving about smoothly and suggestively.*

Text: ***The End.***

Commentary:

• Okay, what do you think? Lucky or yucky? Funny or what?

• Oh well—I suppose this comic strip isn't intended for female readers, is it? And, who knows, perhaps this is the Japanese middle-aged man's secret dream? Urrgh. I just can't imagine that all Japanese middle-aged men would act the way he does. You see, in my opinion, the author likes to capture the degenerate in all of us, or maybe it's just what men think about but don't act out. You be the judge. I'm a woman, so I can't go there.

FLASH!!

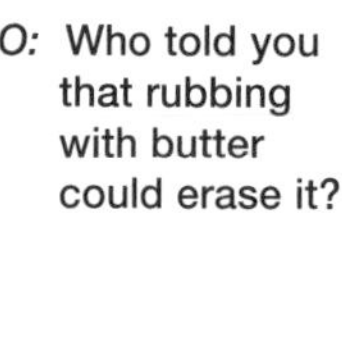

O: Who told you that rubbing with butter could erase it?

f: I say paint thinner would do the trick after all . . .

Commentary:

• This is another elegy, showing deprived youth in search of uncensored material... How desperate they must be.

• The fact is that although it's censored, they did get a hold of a magazine with an attractive looking woman. Too bad they don't understand how complete the censorship is. Oh well, perhaps, this is what being young and male in Japan is all about.

JUDO PAEAN—SINGLE CHRYSANTHEMUM

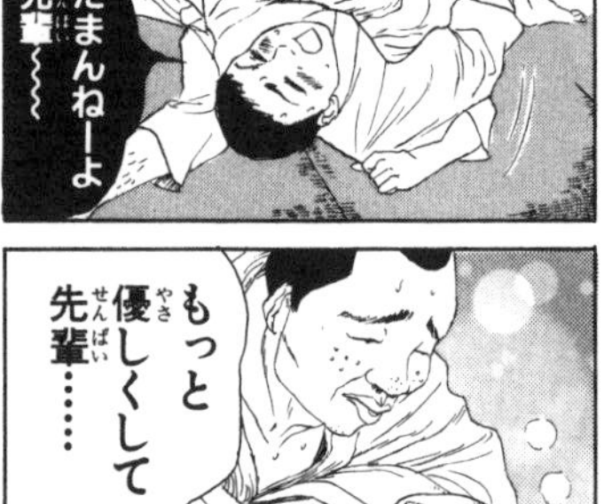

Senpai: Urya, urya!!

Sekimoto: It hurts, Senpai!!

Senpai: Dorya, dorya

Sekimoto: I can't take it, Senpai!!

Sekimoto: Will you be more gentle, Senpai . . .?

Senpai: S—Sekimoto!!

FX: (ba) *A sudden and dramatic move*

Sekimoto: Gyaaah!! Senpai!!

Commentary:

• たまんねーよ (taman-neh-yo) is a colloquial version of たまらないよ (tamara-nai-yo), which means either unbearable, unspeakably wonderful, or troublesome.

• 先輩 (senpai) is a word used for a person who goes to the same school but is in a higher grade or a person who has graduated from the same school ahead of you. 先輩 (senpai) is also used to mean someone who is older, higher in social status, or either academically or artistically superior.

• 関本 (sekimoto) apparently felt the exercise was too painful, but somehow 先輩 (senpai) took it wrong.

• Please note, 菊 (kiku = chrysanthemum) is one of Japan's national flowers, and it inspires various images and symbols in Japan. Nonetheless, in classic Japanese, 菊 (kiku) was used as a metaphor for anus in homosexual relationships.

奴のシュートは地獄だぜ

HIS SHOT IS HELL

Crowd: Ooooooh.

FX: (dogooh) *A loud, hard kick.*

Someone: Goal!!

Crowd: Ooooooh.

Girl 1: Hamichin-kun's great . . .

Girl 2: He's the savior of our soccer team!!

Commentary:

• This is the first of はみちん君 (hamichin-kun) series. はみちん君 (hamichin-kun) is, apparently, one cool dude whom the girls find attractive. However, look closely, and you'll see his testicle sticking out from under his shorts. It is the case in every panel in which he appears—which is not so cool. I have to say, this is a classic example of the author's idiosyncratic sense of humor.

• はみ (hami), in this instance, is short for はみだす (hamidasu) which means to "stick out" or "slip out" ちん (chin) is short for おチンチン (ochinchin) or チンコ (chinko) which are colloquial terms for male genitals. Most little kids know the word おチンチン (ochinchin). 君 (kun) is one of the Japanese suffixes, which is usually used to address a male person who is younger or same age as the speaker. So the name はみちん君 (hamichin-kun) is equivalent to Mr. Slipped Out Ball.

風前の灯

A LIGHT BEFORE THE WIND

Yamagishi: Sensei

Teacher: What's wrong, Yamagishi-kun?

Text: See-Through Love

Yamagishi: Wh— What's this all about!?

Text: ***— To Be Continued—***

Commentary:

• 風前の灯火 (fuuzen no tomoshibi), which translates to read "a light before the wind," is a proverb. It means being in an extremely precarious position. Imagine a small candle that is about to be subjected to a gust of wind—that's exactly what this proverb is referring to.

• It's a scandalous situation for a teacher to have a past where she was a media sensation as a loose woman. And that's why there's this tragic look on the See-Through Teacher's face.

• So the saga of the boy and the See-Through Teacher continues...

㉗サチコとミユキ

(27) SACHIKO AND MIYUKI

Text outside the panel: A manga series: ***Animal Trail***

Miyuki: I am Miyuki, 16 years old.

Miyuki: I usually look plain, but—

Miyuki: I transform at the bar!!

Text: Sachiko is glad to see Miyuki has become a happy child.

㉘サチコとミユキ2

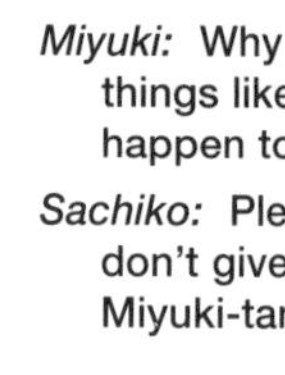

(28) SACHIKO AND MIYUKI 2

Miyuki: Argh, my thing's missing.

Miyuki: Can't believe this.

Miyuki: Who made poo poo in there?

Miyuki: I really can't believe this.

Miyuki: Why do things like this happen to me?

Sachiko: Please don't give up, Miyuki-tan.

Master: You haven't learned yet, you bitch?

Woman: Ouch

Text below the panel: ***To Be Continued***

Commentary:

• It's just that, not too many mothers (be it Japanese or otherwise) would be glad to see their teenage daughters working happily at a bar—wearing skimpy clothes and all.

Commentary:

• As I mentioned earlier, the suffix たん (tan) that follows directly after a person's name, such as Miyuki-tan, is a cute, pre-K kid's way of pronouncing さん (san).

• アマ (尼, ama) means nun, but used in this context, it is an unpleasant way of addressing a woman.

シリーズ
川島日記

某水産会社のパンフに後ろ姿で出ているぜ

みんなでさがそーぜ!!

Series
Kawashima's Diary

Text: A photo of me taken from behind is in the pamphlet of some marine products company.

Slanted text: Let's look for it together!!

Commentary:

• It's a fact that the author used to work for a marine products company as a fishmonger. The pamphlet does actually exists—and if you're so inclined, please do go ahead and look for it.

A MAN WITH SEVEN FACES

七つの顔の男だぜ

Man: That big-faced detective is following us.

Woman: L—Let's shake him off!!

Man: Argh! He read our minds!!

Man: Arrgh!!

Man: Arrrgh!!

Commentary:

• There's a movie called 多羅尾伴内 七つの顔の男だぜ (tarao bannai nanatsuno kaono otoko daze) released in 1960. It is one of the detective 多羅尾伴内 (tarao bannai) series. The detective is played by 片岡千恵蔵 (kataoka chiezou), who was born in 1923 and passed away in 1986. He appeared in 325 films. He started as a 歌舞伎 (kabuki) actor before he launched his successful career in film. The first movie he acted in was made in 1923 and was called 三色すみれ (sanshoku sumire), but it was never released. He is well known as an actor for period pieces (although, this detective series is set in modern Japan). He also played the role of 金さん (kinsan) in the popular TV show 遠山の金さん (tooyama no kinsan).

FAIRYTALE OF KAMOSHIDA

鴨志田メルヘン

Song: Chalalaah Chalalilaah

Song: Zundoko Zundoko Zundoko

Song: Zundoko Zundoko

Song: Zundoko Zundoko

Boy: Clear out, Strip Club!

Text: Baseball.

Boy: Get your morning practice session done over there!!

Commentary:

• 鴨志田 (kamoshida) is a proper noun. メルヘン (meruhen) comes from a German word, Märchen, which means fairytale.

• There are professional baseball players with the last name 鴨志田 (kamoshida), as well as schools with baseball teams named 鴨志田 (kamoshida). 鴨志田 (kamoshida) is also an area in 横浜市 (yokohama-shi), a neighboring city of 川崎 (Kawasaki). The author lives in 川崎 (Kawasaki). It's more likely than not that he used 鴨志田 (kamoshida) of 横浜市 (yokohama-shi).

• Regardless, it is clear that the activity is taking place at a school, and indeed, it's a man's fairytale for a girl's strip club to exist.

THANK YOU

Man: I'll beat you up, you bitch!!

Woman: Gyaaah, you!!

Man: Oops!

Man: I forgot.

Man: Thanks for the past 10 years.

Woman: It's the "Sweet 10 Diamond!!"

Man: I'll beat you up, you bitch!!

Woman: Gyaaah, you!!

HIS PUNCH IS HELL

Boy 1: Ah, what a nice breeze...

FX: (sawa sawa sawa sawa) *A pleasant wind blowing.*

Boy 1: I will defeat you the next time!!

Boy 2: The next time, you'll be sent to hell!!

Boy 1 & 2: Ha ha ha

Boy 1 & 2: Ha ha haha

Boy 1 & 2: Ha ha ha

Girl 1: Hamichin-kun's kind'a cool...

Girl 2: It's the guy thing, isn't it!?

Commentary:

• いてもたろか (itemotaroka) means "I'll beat you up" in Kansai dialect.

• A memorable TV commercial that aired a while back called "Sweet 10 Diamond" captured the imagination of many consumers in Japan. Although it did not succeed in establishing a new tradition, where Japanese couples buy diamonds on their 10th wedding anniversaries, a lot of jewelry in Japan is still sold under the name "Sweet 10 Diamond."

• The husband, apparently a Yakuza, remembers their 10th wedding anniversary, and despite his habitual wife-beating, he takes a moment to give that symbolic piece of jewelry to thank her for staying with him for an entire decade. Maybe this is the TV commercial that was never aired.

Commentary:

• This is another one of theはみちん君 (hamichin-kun) series. Just like the previous episode, his testicle is sticking out from beneath his shorts. Who says he's cool? It's rather embarrassing... Nonetheless, the girls are oblivious (as expected) and can't help being attracted to Mr. Slipped Out Ball.

(29) SACHIKO'S FORTUNE

㉙サチコの幸

Text outside the panel: ***Animal Trail***

Sensei: Congratulations for entering.

FX: (shan shan) *The sound made by the tambourine.*

Sensei: I'm your Sensei and . . .

Sensei: Urgh!!

Sensei: Mama!!

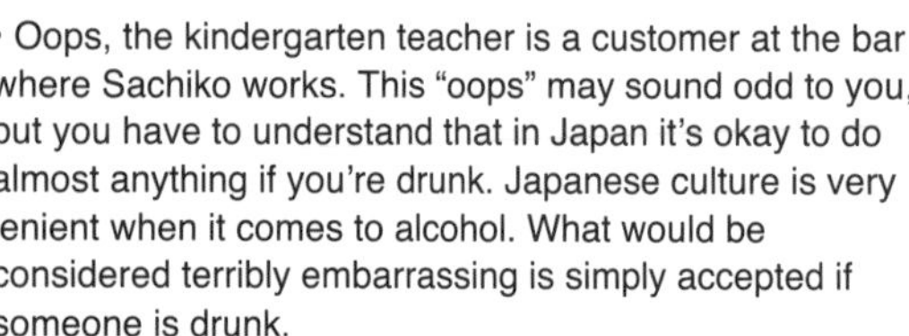

FX: (shan shan shan) *The sound made by the tambourine.*

Sensei: . . .

Text: Sachiko has entered the kindergarten.

Commentary:

• Oops, the kindergarten teacher is a customer at the bar where Sachiko works. This "oops" may sound odd to you, but you have to understand that in Japan it's okay to do almost anything if you're drunk. Japanese culture is very lenient when it comes to alcohol. What would be considered terribly embarrassing is simply accepted if someone is drunk.

• It is often said, "Forget what's been said and done at 酒の席." 酒 (sake) is rice wine, and 席 (seki) is seat(s). So when one's drinking alcohol, others must tolerate his/her behavior. And, of course, that applies to the adult world.

• The first thing that must've come to the Sensei's mind is something embarrassing that he said or did at the bar...

(30) SACHIKO'S FORTUNE 2

㉚サチコの幸2

Sachiko: Sensei, a letter for you.

Text: Momotaro.

Sensei: What!?

Sachiko: Kyaah! ♥

Sensei: W—

Sensei: Wait!!

FX: (totetete) *Rushing away.*

Letter: Your tab is getting big. Sachiko

つづく

Text: Sachiko is trying to draw a distinction between her public and private life.

FX: (zuru . . . zuru . . .) *Slipping down.*

Text below the panel: ***To Be Continued***

Commentary:

• ももたろう (桃太郎, momotaro) is one of the popular folktales that every Japanese kid grows up with. 桃 (momo) means peach, and 太郎 (taro) is a boy's name. ももたろう (momotaro) is also known as "Peach Boy" or "The Legend of Momotaro."

ワカハゲ THE バーバリアン

WAKAHAGE THE BARBARIAN

Old man: Go, Wakahage the Brave!!

Old man: And save the princess!!

Evil man: You've come, Wakahage the Brave.

Brave man: Do you think you can defeat me?!

Princess: You've done it, Wakahage the Brave.

Princess: The evil is destroyed!!

Brave man: Don't call me Wakahage all the time!!

FX: (ban) *A loud slap.*

Commentary:

• ワカハゲ (若禿げ, wakahage) means "the state of being bald while still young." 若い (wakai) means "young," and 禿げる (hageru) means "balding."

• You may wonder why it bothered him that the Princess called him Wakahage the Brave, while he didn't mind it from the old man. I do too. Perhaps, the key is in the title, "Wakahage The Barbarian."

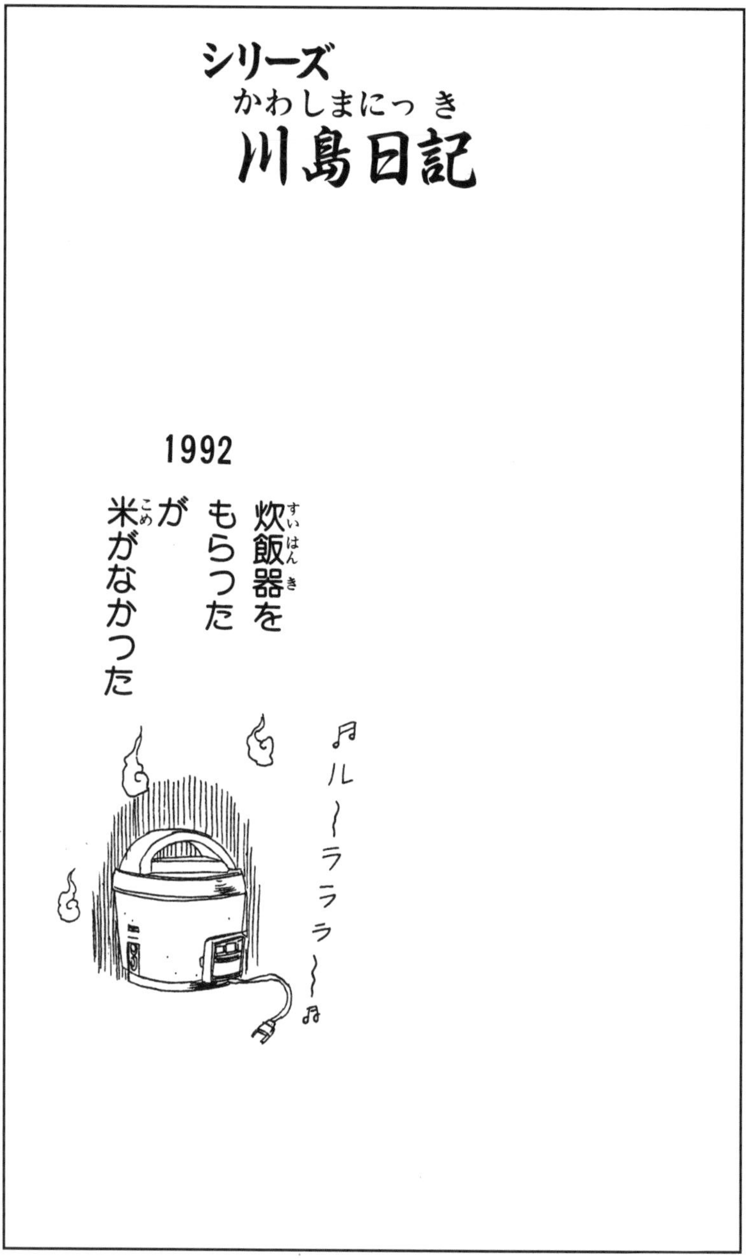

シリーズ

かわしまにっき
川島日記

1992

炊飯器(すいはんき)を
もらった
が
米(こめ)がなかった

♫ル〜ラララ〜♫

Series
Kawashima's Diary

Text: 1992—I received a rice cooker, but I didn't have any rice to cook.

Song: Lu lalalaah

Commentary:

• 炊飯器 (suihanki = rice cooker) is one of the most commonly used household appliances in Japan. Think of TVs and refrigerators. Most households have them—and the popularity and prevalence of 炊飯器 (suihanki) is just as strong.

• The first generation of 炊飯器 (suihanki) was sold commercially in 1953. Ever since, it has evolved with numerous improvements.

となりのさそりちゃん

MY NEIGHBOR SASORI-CHAN

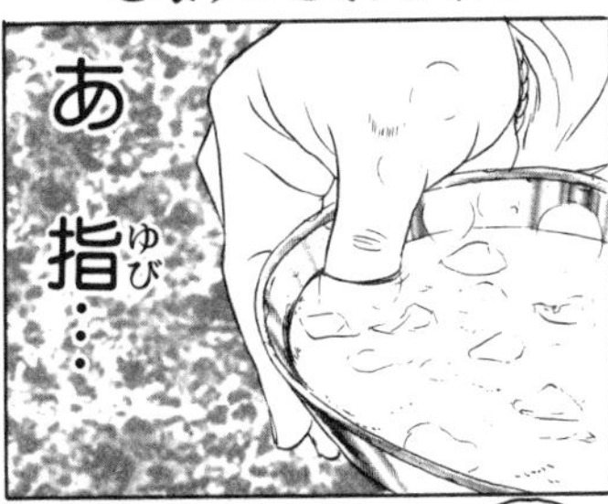

Girl: Ah, the thumb . . .

Girl: I can't believe—

Girl: Urgh!!

Girl: Sasori!!

Text: Bread

Text: My Neighbor Sasori-chan — —- ***The End***

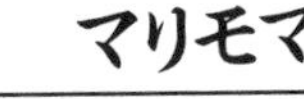

MARIMOMAN

Woman: No!!

Woman: Help me, Marimoman!!

FX: (baaan) *a dramatic presentation*

なんじゃワリャア!!
ドギュ ドギュ ドギュ!!!
マリモマンは弱かった――

Man: What the heck are you!?

FX: (dogyu dogyu dogyu . . .) *a series of gun shots*

Text: Marimoman was weak—

Commentary:

• As I mentioned earlier, there's a movie called 女囚さそり (joshuu sasori = female prisoner, Sasori). The movie was first released in the early 70s. 女囚さそり (joshuu sasori) is a frightening thriller with さそり (sasori) portrayed as a violent fugitive, whose fierceness is beyond imagination.

• This comic strip is the first of theさそりちゃん (sasori-chan) series, where the girl named さそり (sasori) carries a trace of 女囚さそり (joshuu sasori)'s ferociousness.

Commentary:

• マリモ (毬藻, marimo), Cladophora aegagropila, is also known as Algae Balls in the West. It's native to 阿寒湖 (akanko = Lake Akan) in Hokkaido and has been protected as a national monument since 1952. 毬 (mari) means ball and 藻 (mo) refers to algae. It is a type of algae formed by many strings of algae tangled together, forming a fuzzy green ball.

• The plant is free flowing, grows slowly, and some are more than 100 years old. Some smaller Cladophora balls have been observed to grow in freshwater lakes and ponds in European countries, as well as other lakes in Japan. But only in 阿寒湖 (akanko) do they grow to be a large, almost-perfect sphere.

• Here is a picture of a マリモ (marimo):

㉛一年生（ねんせい）

(31) FIRST GRADE STUDENT

Text outside the panel: ***Animal Trail***

Sachiko: Why don't cha look at da photo album,

Sachiko: And then, try and remember.

Sachiko: This and that happened,

Sachiko: don't cha remember . . .?

FX: (horori) *Nostalgic feeling that brings tears to one's eyes.*

Sachiko: In no time, everyone will be . . .

Sachiko: . . . in da first grade.

Woman: (ooi ooi) *Crying.*

Someone: Please give our Mama, Sachiko-san, a big hand!!

FX: (pachi pachi pachi pachi . . .) *Clapping hands.*

Sachiko: Heheh.

Text: Sachiko is entering grade school.

Commentary:

• There's a well-known song called 思い出のアルバム (omoide no alubamu = Album of Recollections), which became popular after it was sung on a TV show called みんなのうた (minna no uta = Everyone's Song) on NHK in 1982. It has become a standard song that is sung at kindergarten graduation ceremonies. Please note, in Japan, kindergarten is still optional for kids to attend, and officially, schooling starts with the 1st grade.

• In this comic strip, you can see another example of 泣き上戸 (naki jogo), a person who starts crying once he/she gets drunk.

• へへー (heheh) is a shy, suppressed sort of giggle.

㉜一年生（ねんせい）2

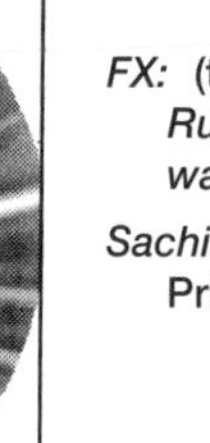

(32) FIRST GRADE STUDENT 2—

FX: (totetete . . .) *Rushing forward.*

Sachiko: Principal!!

Principal: Ha ha ha, what's up, Sacchan?

FX: (shu) *The sound of turning the lighter on.*

Sachiko: Your tab is getting big.

Text: ***Animal Trail, Part I —- The End***

Commentary:

• こおちょーてんてー (koocho tentee) is 校長先生 (koucho sensei) said in baby talk.

• Oops, how embarrassing, if you know what I mean...

TOMORROW NEVER COMES

Man: Ugh..

Man: This singer's voice . . .

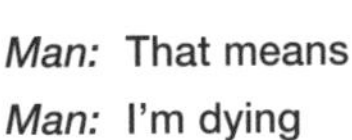

Man: That means

Man: I'm dying . . .

FX: (hyooi hyooi) *Hopping around.*

Commentary:

• If you're a metal head, you can probably understand the reason why the author drew the likeness of Ronnie James Dio in this elfin (and somewhat demonic) image and renamed him Jonnie James Deo. In the late 60s, Ronnie James Dio was playing with a band called Electric Elves, which eventually changed its name to Elf. He also released numerous albums with demonic imagery in the 1970s and 80s. Remember Rainbow, Black Sabbath and DIO. They were all his babies.

• "Tomorrow never comes" is from the song "Die Young," released by Black Sabbath.

• The Yakuza man has realized that he's dying after seeing the demonic image of RJD—a somewhat twisted version of Grim Reaper, don't you think? If you recognize RJD, you may either laugh, be dismayed, or say "so?"

DYNAMITE FELLA

Man: Someone!!

Man: Please put out my dynamite!!

Man: Please put out the fuse!!

FX: (joro joro) *The sound of spurting urine.*

Man: Humph, it's put out . . .

Man: My furichin saved me.

Commentary:

• フリチン (furichin) is a slang for "the state of man's nakedness." チン (chin) is, as I described earlier, is short for おチンチン (ochinchin) or チンコ (chinko), which are colloquial terms for male genitals. As to the フリ (furi) part of the word, there are a couple of opinions as to how the slang came about. One opinion is フリ (furi) comes from the word 振る (furu), which means to swing. In this case, another slang フルチン (furuchin) is interchangeable with フリチン (furichin). The second opinion is that フリ (furi) comes from the English word "free" and フル (furu) comes from "full." So, in this case, フリチン (furichin) refers to the free state of the male genitals (i.e. they can move about freely without the underwear), while フルチン (furuchin) refers to male genital in full view.

フリチン野郎

FURICHIN FELLA

Boy: From a school like this,

Boy: I'll leave on my own accord.

Boy: So long!!

FX: (do do do do do) *A loud sound reminiscent of a stampede.*

Text: Furichin Fella, Episode 1—

FX: (do do do do do) *A loud sound reminiscent of a stampede.*

Text: Furichin Expelled from School —— ***The End***

Commentary:

• In this comic strip, the author is poking fun at the 学園ヒーロー (gakuen hiiro = school hero) prevalent in the 学園ドラマ (gakuen dorama = school drama), which is a type of dramatic series about students that was popular in the early 1970s. It is a genre focused on youth and their struggles at school.

シリーズ
かわしまにっき
川島日記

冷凍庫（れいとうこ）に
閉（と）じこめ
られたこと
ありますか？

Series
Kawashima's Diary

Text: Have you ever been shut up inside a freezer?

Commentary:

• This must be another experience the author had as a fishmonger—at least that's my guess.

①鉄火場仁義(てっかばじんぎ)

←"けものみち"第二部、"こわれもの"スタート!!

※注：登場人物に変更ありません。

(1) GAMING ROOM MORAL CODE

Vertical text with an arrow: ***"Animal Trail"*** Part II, *"Breakable"* starts!! * Note: Characters remain the same.

Text outside the panel: Breakable

FX: (pote pote) *Baby walk.*

Sachiko: Thank you for always looking after Yoko-tan.

FX: (pekori) *Deep bow.*

Sachiko: I'm embarrassed.

FX: (doki doki) *Throbbing heart.*

Girl: Yoko-chan's Mama is so cute! ♥

Commentary:

• 鉄火場 (tekkaba) means a "gambler's den." 仁義 (jingi) means "a morale code or honor."

• There's a movie called 鉄火場仁義 (tekkaba jingi) released in 1966. It's a drama involving a father, who joins the Yakuza and becomes a gambler, and his son, who goes after his father for revenge. In a surprise turn of events, the father dies as he saves his son at the 鉄火場 (tekkaba).

• You may know that the tuna sushi roll is called 鉄火巻 (tekka maki) in Japanese. The name comes from the fact that tuna rolls were typically offered at the 鉄火場 (tekkaba). It makes sense because 鉄火巻 (tekka maki) are easy to handle and eat while gambling.

②鉄火場勝負(てっかばしょうぶ)

つづく

(2) GAMING ROOM MATCH

FX: (waa waa) *The noise of the excited crowd.*

FX: (totetete) *Rush along.*

Text: 1st Grade, Sachiko

FX: [waa waa] *The noise of the excited crowd.*

Yoko: You'll try again next year . . .

Sachiko: Heheh.

Yoko: So, let's have some lunch.

Sachiko: Kyaaah

Girl: Yoko-chan's Mama is so cute!

Text below the panel: ***To Be Continued.***

Commentary:

• This comic strip shows a typical 運動会 (undokai) held annually at Japanese schools. 運動会 (undokai) is an all-day sports event, where students compete in various sports.

• It often takes place on Sundays so that families can come to watch with picnic lunches.

俺が地獄の手品師ダ (おれ じごく てじなし)

AM THE MAGICIAN FROM HELL

Cockroach: Oops, that's enough, you guys!

Man: What?

FX: (vu vu vu vu) *A buzzing sort of sound.*

FX: (vu vu vu) *A buzzing sort of sound.*

Someone: Cockroach Cop!!

Text: The Cockroach Cop was . . .

Text: . . . for some reason, despised by everyone.—The End

Commentary:

• There is a movie called ゴキブリ刑事 (gokiburi deka), which translates to "Cockroach Cop." The movie is based on a manga series with the same title. The film was released in 1973. In the movie, a cop (the hero) called the gangsters ゴキブリ (gokiburi = cockroaches), as he relentlessly pursued and captured them.

• In this comic strip, the author made fun of the title and created a new character, the cop, who can transform into a real cockroach.

さそりちゃん

SASORI-CHAN

Man: You're still not telling me, Sasori?

Man: Where's Yoriko's indoor shoes?

FX: (baki baki baki) *The sound of a series of loud blows.*

Man: Tell me!! Where'd you hide them?

FX: (niyari) *Grin.*

Man: Eek!!

Text: Sasori-chan —— ***To Be Continued***

Commentary:

• As I've mentioned, the author took the frightening image of the violent fugitive called さそり (sasori) from the movie 女囚さそり (joshuu sasori) and created his own version of scary girl さそりちゃん (sasori-chan) in Gloom Party.

• This comic strip may give you some idea what 女囚さそり (joshuu sasori) is really like.

POSITIONING IN SUMMER

Man: I am the new candidate

FX: (jiri jiri) *Burning hot.*

Man: OX of Jimintoh.

Name: Kawao OX

Man: . . . pressed Japan . . . political belief.

FX: (jiri jiri) *Burning hot.*

Name: Kawao OX

FX: (jiri jiri) *Burning hot.*

Man: . . . pan style . . . is necessary

Man: . . . tion as a whole . . . onsensus

FX: (jiri jiri) Burning hot.

FX: (fura fura) Swing back and forth.

Name: Kawao

FX: (jiri jiri) Burning hot.

Man: . . . please . . . your support

Woman: The heat is making my dad groggy . . .

Woman: Do your best . . .

Commentary:

• Urrgh, the フリチン (furichin)!! Please read the comic strip entitled “DYNAMITE FELLA” for an explanation of what フリチン (furichin) is.

シリーズ
かわしまにっき
川島日記

Series Kawashima's Diary

生イクラ作らせたら
誰にも負けない
マンガ家だぜ

Text: Although I'm a manga artist, I can prepare fresh salmon roe better than anyone else—if not just as well.

Commentary:

- And, we know why.
- BTW, regarding 生イクラ (nama ikura), 生 (nama) literary means fresh or raw, and イクラ (ikura) means salmon roe. Many people think of 生イクラ (nama ikura) as uncooked salmon roe. However, the fact is that 生イクラ (nama ikura) means "fresh" (uncooked) salmon roe that have nothing added to them and have never been frozen. In other words, uncooked, fresh salmon roe that's been frozen or had some salt added are not called 生イクラ (nama ikura).
- Salmon roe continue to breathe for about eight hours after the salmon is captured. Supposedly, it's best to use that window of opportunity to prepare them. It is common to use salt or soy sauce to prepare 生イクラ (nama ikura). Sushi chefs usually choose salt.

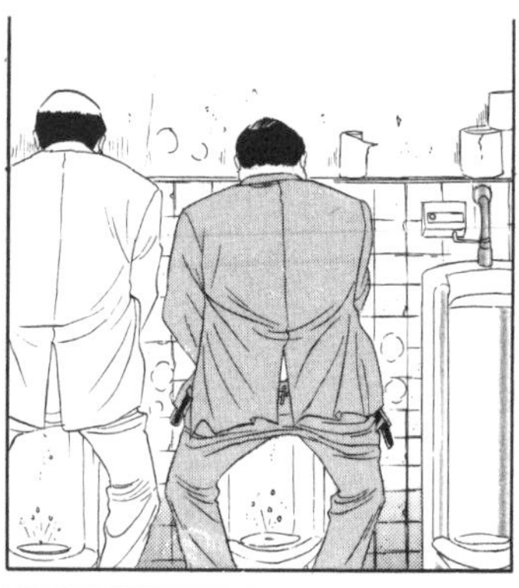

Man 1: Huh? Where's Super-Long Urinating Section Chief?

Man 2: He's still in there . . .

Commentary:

• しょんべん (shonben) is slang for urine.

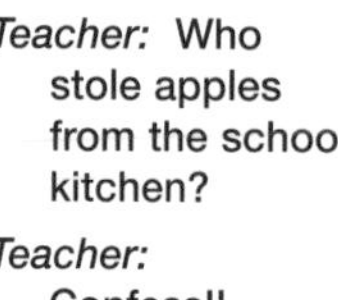

APPLE SONG

Teacher: Who stole apples from the school kitchen?

Teacher: Confess!!

FX: (zawa zawa zawa zawa) *Noise of the crowd.*

Teacher: Scary girl, Sasori . . .

Text: Sasori-chan of apples —— ***The End***

Commentary:

• りんごのさそりちゃん (ringo no sasori-chan) is an odd phrase. If it's written さそりちゃんのりんご (sasori-chan no ringo), it translates to "Sasori-chan's apple." However, since the position of さそりちゃん (sasori-chan) is swapped with the りんご (ringo = apple), it translates to read "apples' Sasori-chan" or "Sasori-chan of apples." It's as if Sasori-chan belongs to the apples.

• Anyhow, please focus on the stubborn and severe look on さそりちゃん (sasori-chan) as well as the reaction from the teacher. That's what makes this girl special.

A NIGHT IN HAWAII

Boy: I'm happy.

FX: (hori hori) *A scratching sound, as well as a sound of getting attention.*

ボカァ君といる時が
一番幸せなんだ
ふたりを〜〜〜〜
ゆーやみんが〜

Boy: I'm the happiest when I'm with you.

Song: Under the twilight on the beach, the two of us are . . .

イカスわぁ
はみちん君…
我が校の
プリンスね

Girl 1: Hamichin-kun's so cool . . .

Girl 2: He's the prince of our school, isn't he?

Commentary:

• There's a popular song called 君といつまでも (kimi to itsumademo) which translates to read "with you forever" by 加山雄三 (kayama yuzo). The song was first released in 1965 and became a big hit, with over 3 million copies sold. It's considered one of the representative songs by the artist. The words uttered and sung by the boy in the first three panels of this comic strip are the exact words found in that song.

• And, oops, as his name indicates, はみちん君 (hamichin-kun) is still showing his private parts—and yet again, the girls don't notice, or do they? Maybe this explains his popularity...?

そこまでよっ

THAT'S ENOUGH

Woman: That's enough, you guys!!

Woman: The Bondage Girl

Woman: is here!!

FX: (doh) *A loud thud.*

く…
くるしい
モガ
モガ
ボンデージガール終

Woman: It's—It's painful.

Text: The end of the Bondage Girl.

Commentary:

• Apparently, images of bondage girls were published as early as the 1940s in America by the fetish-photographer John Willie. After a crackdown, these images went underground for a long period of time, only to reappear in public in the 1970s. They were published in magazines through the 90s. Nowadays, however, since the Internet has become so popular, they mostly appear online.

• The word ボンデージガール (bondeeji gaaru = bondage girl) is an imported word from English, which probably came into general use after the Web became popular. This comic strip is, obviously, inspired by this relatively new (and hip) term.

③母心 (ははごころ)

(3) MOTHER'S HEART

Text outside the panel: Breakable

Sachiko: I just got back from shopping.

Sachiko: (haa haa) Huffing hard.

Yoko: Okay.

Yoko: What's this ice cream doing here!?

Yoko: It's not okay to waste money!!

Yoko: Go back and return it right away.

Sachiko: (e u u) *A sobbing sound.*

Girl: Yoko, your Mama's so cute! ♥

④猫おどり (ねこ)

(4) CAT DANCE

Song: I'm a cat.

Song: Meow, meow, meow!♥

Girl: Ah, Sacchan.

Sachiko: Meow!

Miyuki: Where are you, Nee-san?

Sachiko: Meow!

Text: Because Sachiko has become a first grader, she has changed her image. — ***—The End***

Song: Meow, meow, meow.

Commentary:

• Just like the words 男心 (otoko gokoro), which represents the generally understood sentiment of men, and 女心 (onna gokoro), which represents a women's sentiment, 母心 (haha gokoro) is the word that represents a sentiment commonly shared by mothers.

• What's funny about this comic strip is that Sachiko's 母心 (haha gokoro) is certainly not understood by Yoko, the daughter. But really, Sachiko's sentiment isn't really a mother's, now is it?

Commentary:

• イメチェン (ime chen) comes from the English words "image change," which has become a common term in Japan.

• So, instead of the raccoon-like animal called タヌキ (tanuki), she's a cat now...

ない!!

MISSING!!

Man: Urgh, the toilet paper's missing!

Man: Hey, is there anyone out there?

Man: Huh?

Man: Sasori!!

Man: E—Eek...

FX: (ata futa) *Fuss about blindly without knowing what else to do.*

Text: Sasori-chan of the toilet —

— The End

りんごの歌2

APPLE SONG 2

FX: (koro koro) *Rolling away.*

FX: (koro koro koro koro) *Rolling away.*

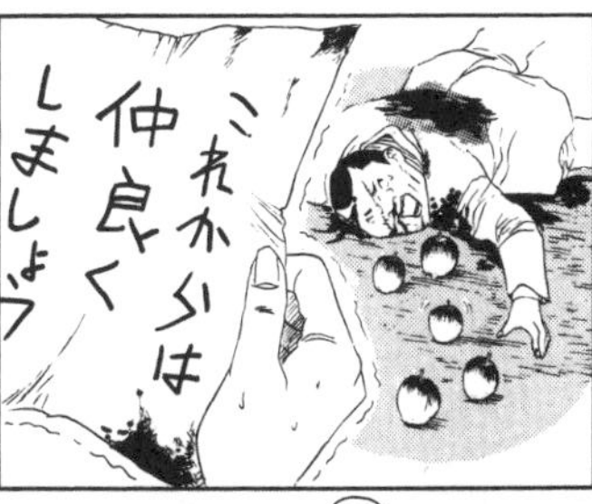

Text: Let's be friends from now on.

Man: . . .

Text: Gongitsune Yakuza —- ***The End***

Commentary:

• トイレのさそりちゃん (toire no sasori-chan) is another odd phrase. If it's written さそりちゃんのトイレ (sasori-chan no toire), it translates to "Sasori-chan's toilet." However, since the position of さそりちゃん (sasori-chan) is swapped with the トイレ (toire = toilet), it translates to read "toilet's Sasori-chan" or "Sasori-chan of the toilet." It's as if Sasori-chan belongs to the toilet.

• Please take note of the image of the toilet in panel #2. It's one of the common styles of flush toilets in Japan. Here's a picture of the toilet:

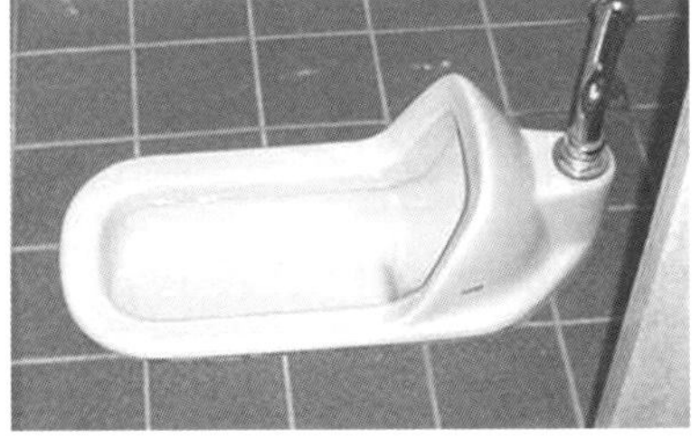

Commentary:

• ゴンギツネ (gongitsune) is a well known Japanese folktale about a fox called ゴンギツネ (gongitsune). In the story, a parentless, friendless fox, ゴンギツネ (gongitsune), plays a trick on the others (perhaps, out of loneliness). One day, the fox encounters a man fishing. As usual, he plays a trick on the man by letting go of all the fish and stealing the eels. A few days later, the fox witnesses a funeral, where the man is burying his mother. The fox realizes that the man was fishing for his sick mother. Seeing how the man became parentless and lonely (like the fox himself), ゴンギツネ (gongitsune) repents and, to make up for the wrong he's done, secretly brings nuts and other food from the mountain to the man's house. The man doesn't know who has brought the food and wonders if it is a gift from heaven. Then one day the man sees ゴンギツネ (gongitsune) approaching his house, and he thinks that the fox has come to play another trick on him. Without hesitation, he shoots the fox, killing it—only to discover what the fox has brought him.

CONFERENCE IN PROGRESS

Man 1: . . . That's all, and therefore,

Man 1: we need marketing research and

FX: (soro soro soro) *Slowly and quietly.*

Man 1: ***Arrgh!!***

FX: (bi bi bi) *An intense pain shoots through —like an electric current.*

Man 1: A flexible rationalization!!

Man 1: . . . must . . . be . . . d—done . . .

FX: (jin jin jin . . .) *Pain reaching a numbing intensity.*

Man 1: Consumer's . . . needs must . . .

Man 2: That Sharp Piles Division Chief is sharp, isn't he?

Man 3: I bet he'll get the Vice Section Chief's post.

Commentary:

• キレる (kireru) means sharp in different ways, such as having a smart/keen mind, as well as having a sharp edge to cut. 痔 (ji) means piles, and obviously, the Division Chief is suffering from piles. The author is making fun of the 課長 (kacho), the Division Chief, by naming him キレ痔課長 (kireji kacho) -- one who is both smart, as well as in pain due to his bleeding piles.

WHAT DOES BEAUTY MEAN TO GRADE SCHOOL KIDS?

Boy 1: Panties...

Boy 2: Yup...

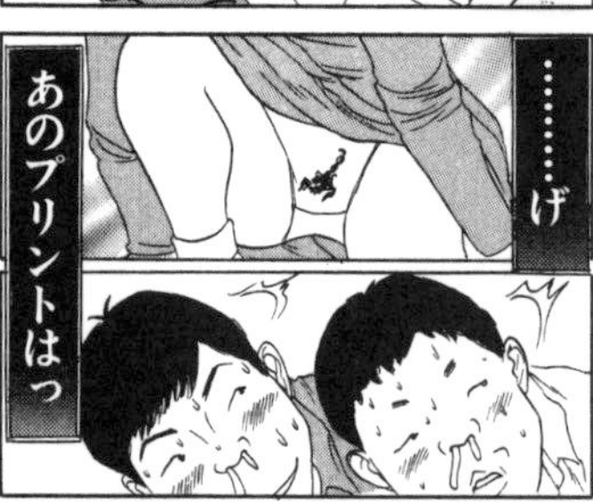

Boy 1: ...Urrgh

Boy 2: That mark.

Boys: Sasori!!

Boys: Eeeek!!

Text: Sexy Sasori-chan —— ***The End***

Commentary:

• So, what does beauty mean to grade school kids? Obviously the printed scorpion on the girl's panties certainly isn't beautiful—especially when the girl isさそりちゃん (sasori-chan).

• Please note the author's trademark, blushing cheeks, not only on the boys but also on さそりちゃん (sasori-chan). The blushing cheek often represents a quality of 恥じらい (hajirai), which is a feeling of shyness, bashfulness or naiveté. Japanese males tend to find it attractive when a female possesses the quality of 恥じらい (hajirai). So, despite the reaction of the boys in this comic strip, I'd say that this さそりちゃん (sasori-chan) in panel #4 might appear rather cute to many Japanese readers.

ENSOKU

えんそく
遠足

FX: (joro joro joro . . .) *The sound of spurting urine.*

Boy: . . .

FX: (njojojojo) *The sound of spurting urine.*

Boy: . . .

せんせェ～
頻尿くんがいません～
またかよう

Girl: Sensei, Hinnyo-kun's missing.

Sensei: Again?

Commentary:

• 遠足 (ensoku) is a common school event in Japan. It is similar to field trips in America. Usually, 遠足 (ensoku) is an all day event, which entails visiting far away places like shrines, great historical ruins, natural reserves, etc. Students bring snacks, drinks and picnic lunches to 遠足 (ensoku). Students are commonly equipped with backpacks, water flasks, hats and uniforms (like the gym clothes shown here).

• The author is making fun of a boy who needs to urinate frequently by calling him 頻尿くん (hinnyo kun). 頻 (hin) represents "frequent," and 尿 (nyo) represents "urine."

MATSUDA

松田～～～ッ
出てこい～～～ッ
まつだ
松田
銃なんか捨てて出てこいよっ

Shigeno: Matsuda!! Come on out!!

Shigeno: Throw away your gun and come on out!!

俺だよ
わかるか!?
同じ畜産科だった
重野だよ

Shigeno: It's me. Can you see me!?

Shigeno: I'm Shigeno. I attended the Class of Stockbreeding with you.

おぼえてっぺ
おめと一緒ぬ…
豚で初体験した
重野だッ!!

Shigeno: You remember, don't you? Together, we . . .

Shigeno: lost our virginity with the pigs. I'm that Shigeno!!

FX: (dogyuun) *The sound of a loud gun shot.*

Text: ***The End***

Commentary:

• I'll leave it up to you why Matsuda shot himself to death. I think it's pretty obvious.

シネスコ版 昭和の青春

CINEMA SCOPE VERSION, SEISHUN OF SHOWA

Melody: Cha la laaah, cha la li laah, cha la la
Text: Niggatsu Romantic Porn

Woman: Stop it, Sensei!!
Woman: Please stop it!!

Woman: No, don't!!

Text: ***The End***

Commentary:

• 昭和 (showa) is an era that extends from 1926 through 1988. 日活ロマンポルノ (nikkatsu roman poruno) is an actual porn producer, who began releasing porn movies in 1971. They produced over 1,100 porn movies through 1988. Obviously, the author wrote にっがつロマンポルノ (niggatsu roman poruno) with 日活ロマンポルノ (nikkatsu roman poruno) in mind.

Woman: That's enough, you guys!!

FX: (kara kara . . . kara kara . . .) A rattling sound.

Woman: The Bondage Gal . . .

Woman: . . . is here!!

Woman: It's—It's painful.

Text: The end of the Bondage Gal.

Text below the panel: "Gloom Party" vol. 1, ***The End***

Commentary:

• This is the second episode of the Bondage Girl series. This time the woman is called Bondage Gal, but it is the same gag. Please see the comic strip entitled THAT'S ENOUGH for additional commentary.

End of Volume—Bonus Part 1

"A collection of words spoken by related parties"

- To commemorate the issuance of this book, we put together some of the comments Mr. Kawashima has received from various people over time.

"I read it every week, although it makes me grumpy." *April 1995, a male neighbor.*

"Ah . . . Watanabe-san (the real name of Mr. Kawashima), your manga? Yes, I know of it. You're really ecchi, aren't you?" *January 1995, a female part-time worker at Tama Branch of Y Marine Products.*

"Since you quit, our sales volume has increased a lot, you know . . ." *May 1995, Mr. O, Kawashima's former boss at Tama Branch of Y Marine Products.*

"If you write random things once too many times, I'll ban you from entering this place!!" *July 1995, Branch Manager at Tama Branch of Y Marine Products.*

"Ho ho ho ho ho ho . . . I haven't read . . ." February 1996, a neighborhood housewife.

"What!? That's the Mr. Kawashima? That foppish person . . .?" *August 1995, a female receptionist at A-ta Shoten.*

"I won't forgive you if you dare say you've become poorer than the time you were a fishmonger." *December 1994, Mr. O, the Editor in Chief of X Magazine (during the end of the year party).*

"Ah, that four-panel comic strip . . . Is that supposed to be a gag or what? Hmm." *October 1995, some high school student (on the Sobu Line train)*

"So, what's this Sacchan all about? I don't get it at all." *September 1995, possibly a middle-age man (a phone call received by the editor's office).*

End of Volume— Bonus Part 2

"Recording of stray thoughts over photos"

• We put together memorable thoughts over photos which Mr. Kawashima diligently gathered as reference material for his drawings.

▶ **First Photo:** My neighborhood is a stage for the "Pastoral Depression" of Haruo Sato. Wrong? Basically, it's peaceful countryside.

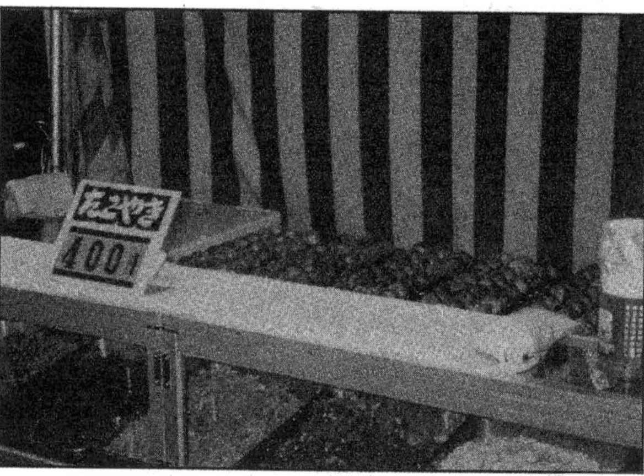

▲ **Second Photo:** Takoyaki stand in front of X train station of the Odakyu private line. You won't witness the scene described in the comic strip entitled "AARN♥" here.

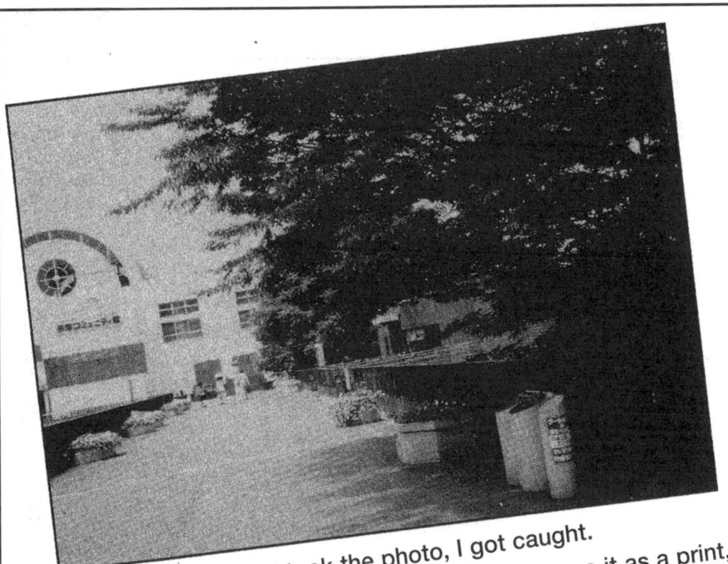

The moment after I took the photo, I got caught.
Since it's very small, you may not be able to see it as a print, but the fact is, I noticed after the film was developed that a police officer was staring at me...

Conversation:

"You... must be an extreme leftist!!!"

"No, you're mistaken!"

"Then, why are you taking a picture of the police station!!?"

"Because I draw pictures."

"Pictures!!? You...what's your occupation!!?"

"A fishmonger."

"You ass... you've got no respect, do you!!?"

— Dark Change — Curtain

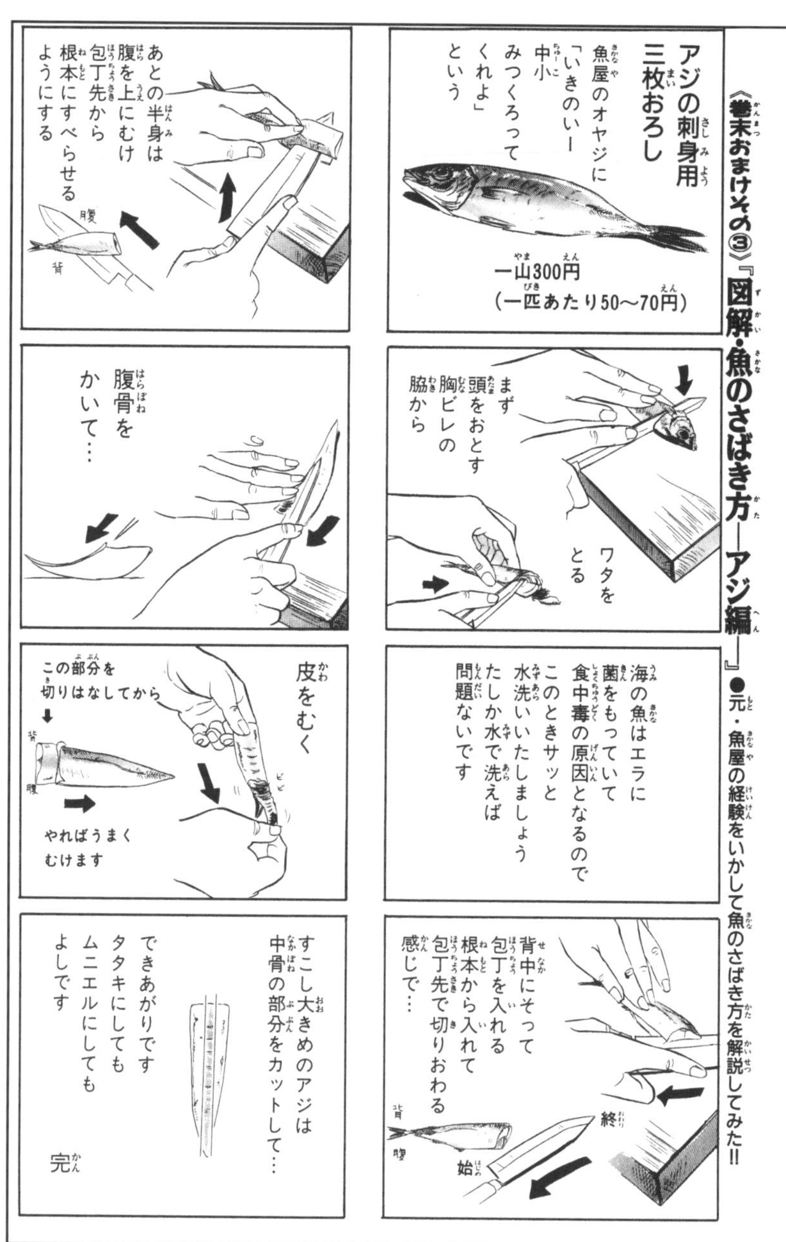

End of Volume—Bonus Part 3

"Illustration • proper handling of fish—mackerel edition—"

• As a former fishmonger, I tried to illustrate how to handle fish properly here!!

1—Mackerel for Sashimi.

Three Piece Cut

First, tell the fishmonger, "please get me fresh Chuko mackerel."

300 yen per mound (about 50 to 70 yen per fish)

2—Next, slice the head off, then from under the breast fin, take out the intestines.

3—Fish from the ocean have bacteria that can cause food poisoning, so you must quickly rinse it with water. If I remember correctly, so long as you wash with water, you shouldn't have any problems.

4—Insert the knife along the back. Make sure to start with the root of the knife and finish with the tip of the knife...

終 = finish

始 = start

背 = back

腹 = stomach

5—With the remaining half, flip the fish so that the stomach is facing up. Use the tip of the knife and slide it down so as to finish with the root of the knife.

腹 = stomach

背 = back

6—Scrape off the stomach bones...

7—Then, peel off the skin.

If you try after you cut this apart, you should have no problem peeling it off.

8—If the mackerel is somewhat big, cut off the middle bones.

There, it's all done. Perfect not only for Sashimi but also for Tataki or Meuniere.

The End

Y Marine Products' Trade Secret: Fried Mackerel Cut

The Chuko mackerels sold in early spring have a lot of bones and are not fit for grilling. They're better to deep fry.

2—First, get rid of the ragged end. By inserting the knife from below, it comes off cleanly.

3—Cut off the head and take out the intestines. The intes-tines taste bitter if left there...

4—Like the illustration, pull open the half side of the fish.

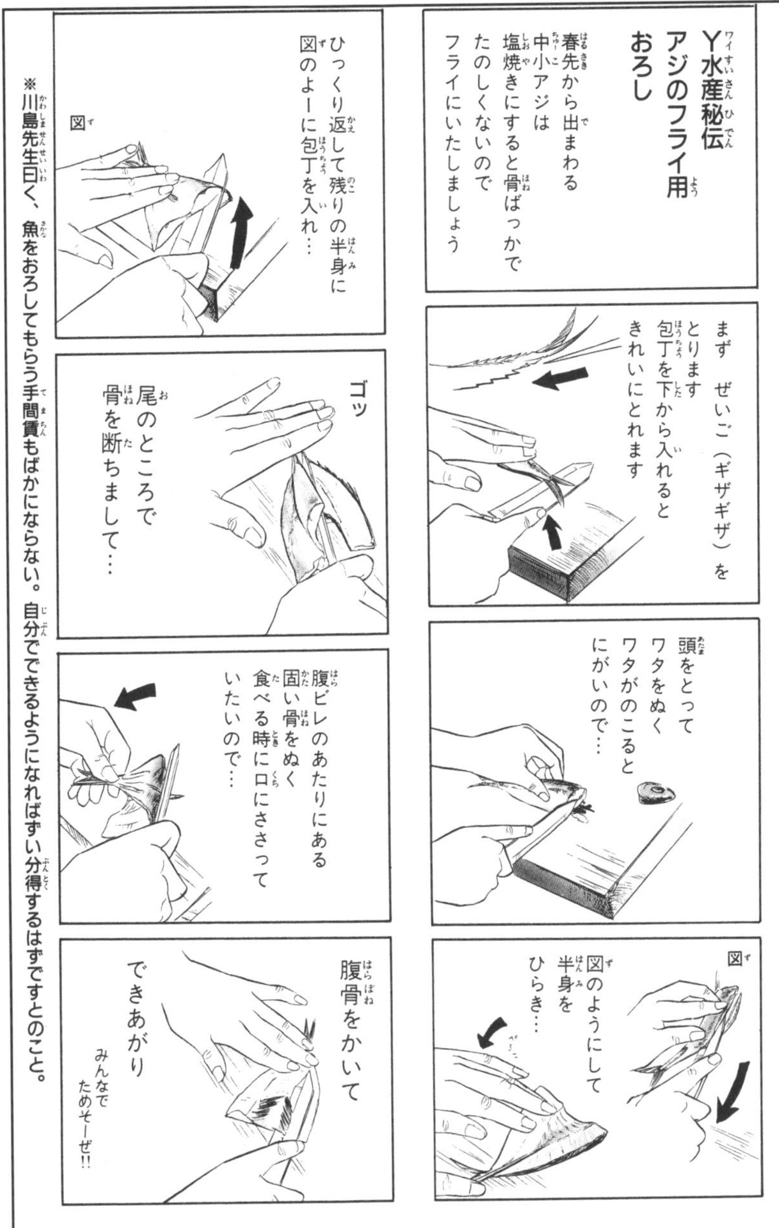

5—Then, turn the fish over and insert the knife into the remaining half side just like the illustration.

6—With a good push, cut off the bone at the tail...

7—Then take out the bone by the stomach fin. If you don't, it'll hurt when you eat it.

8—Once you scrape off the stomach bones, it's all done. Why don't you try doing this!!

Note outside the panel: According to Mr. Kawashima, the fishmonger charges a good fee to prepare a fish. He believes that once you learn how to do it, you can save some money.

End of Volume— Bonus Part 4

"Forgotten Masterpieces"

- Big budget films are not the only movies!! Here are Mr. Kawashima's four favorite movies from among the films produced by Shin Toho, whose films Mr. Kawashima adores.

"Onna Gankutsuoh"

「女巌窟王」

("The Count of Monte Cristo," by Alexander Dumas, is known as 巌窟王 (gankutsuoh) in Japanese. This movie's title sounds a lot like "The Count of Monte Cristo," with a woman as the protagonist.)

Produced in 1960

- Director: Yoshiki Onoda
- Actors: Yoko Mihara, Masayo Banri, Teruo Yoshida

It's the film that was the talk of the town, with Shin Toho's golden trio as the main characters. The scene that should capture your attention is where Mihara and Banri dance.

I love Masayo Banri. Her representative works "Boryoku Musume," "Boryoku Gonin Musume," and "Kaidan Ama Yurei" are not on video yet. It's really unfortunate. By the way, I don't remember... the story of this film...

"Jouoh Bachi No Ikari"

(Wrath of the Queen Bee)

Produced in 1958—

- Director: Teruo Ishii
- Actors: Naoko Kubo, Bunta Sugawara, Ken Utsui

Boss Yuri rages with burning wrath at the harbor. Naoko Kubo's ardent performance shines in this great hit film series.

Naoko Kubo is featured in this film. (I'm afraid I haven't researched what other films she has appeared in.) "Hurricane Masa," the lone wolf performed by Ken Utsui, is incredibly cool!! But, again...I don't remember... what kind of story it was.

"Jouoh Bachi To Daigaku No Ryuu"

「女王蜂と大学の竜」

(Queen Bee and Ryuu of Daigaku)

Produced in 1960

- Director: Teruo Ishii
- Actors: Yoko Mihara, Kanjuro Arashi, Shigeru Amachi

Jouoh Bachi is the queen bee, who can bring tears to men's eyes, and Daigaku No Ryuu is the ex-commando. Together they go on a rampage in this exciting action thriller.

Yoko Mihara took on the role of Yakuza's big sister. Another impressive film in which she appeared is, of course, "Joshuu #701 • Sasori." Story...? I don't remember.

"Onna Doreisen"

「女奴隷船」

(Female Slave Ship)

Produced in 1960

- Director: Yoshiki Onoda
- Actors: Bunta Sugawara, Utako Mitsuya, Yoko Mihara

What's attractive about this film is the appearance of superstars like Bunta Sugawara, Tetsuro Tanba and Utako Mitsuya, as well as the showy action scenes set in the ocean.

According to "Norainu No Onnen, Bunta Sugawara," this film is the seventh movie he appeared in after his debut. Apparently, this is the only film that's been brought to video for circulation. Tetsuro Tanba appeared as a slave-trader—a totally pigeonholed role for him... I don't remember the story.

- I selected four films out of my personal collection, and it's almost as if I'm bragging about my treasures. If I get another opportunity to do something like this, I'd like to mention masterpieces covering a much wider range.

Pictures provided by: Clarion Soft

Let's Draw
MANGA™ 漫画
ALL ABOUT
FIGHTING
Draw
MANGA 漫画
ALL ABOUT
FIGHTING
By
MAKOTO NAKAJIMA &
BIG MOUTH FACTORY
AVAILABLE NOW!!
BY MAKOTO NAKAJIMA
& BIG MOUTH FACTORY
ISBN# 1-56970-987-4 $19.95
Distributed Exclusively by:
WATSON-GUPTILL PUBLICATIONS
770 Broadway
New York, NY 10003
www.watsonguptill.com
DMP
Digital Manga Publishing
DIGITAL MANGA PUBLISHING
www.dmpbooks.com

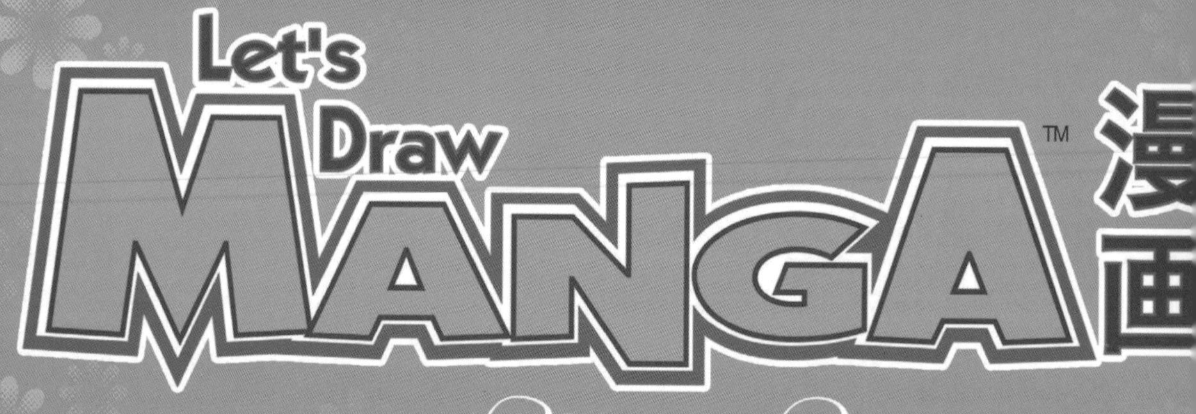

Shoujo Characters

Draw shoujo manga the way you like it!

TEE HEE

ISBN# 1-56970-966-1 SRP $19.95

Both beginner and intermediate artists can now learn to draw "shoujo" characters in the highly recognizable styles established by celebrated Japanese manga artists. With detailed coverage of classic characteristics and basic features, including signature costumes, hairstyles and accessories, this book is a dream come true for the aspiring "shoujo" manga artist.

Distributed Exclusively by:
Watson-Guptill Publications
770 Broadway
New York, NY 10003
www.watsonguptill.com

www.dmpbooks.c

Let's Draw MANGA™ 漫画

TOKYO URBAN-HIP HOP CULTURE

ISBN# 1-56970-969-6
$19.95

Distributed Exclusively by:
WATSON-GUPTILL PUBLICATIONS
770 Broadway
New York, NY 10003
www.watsonguptill.com

DIGITAL MANGA PUBLISHING
www.dmpbooks.com

READY …
SET …
COLOR!

DISCOVER THE TRUE NATURE OF COLOR AND THE BEST WAYS TO ADD COLOR TO YOUR DRAWINGS. TAKE STEP-BY-STEP LESSONS ON COLORING LINE DRAWINGS USING PAINT, INK, MARKERS, COMPUTERS AND MANY OTHER KINDS OF MEDIA. LEARN TO USE COLOR LIKE THE PROS, AND YOU'LL NEVER BE SATISFIED WITH BLACK-AND-WHITE LINES AGAIN!

Let's Draw MANGA 漫画 USING COLOR

FREE OFFER from COPIC while supplies last!! see inside for details

JOHN OTT · YOU KUSANO

AVAILABLE NOW

ISBN 1-56970-988-

$19.95

Digital Manga Publishing
www.dmpbooks.com